We Run This House

We Run This House

THE GIRLS' GUIDE TO FLAG FOOTBALL

AnnaSofia Dickens

Copyright © 2025 by AnnaSofia Dickens

No part of this publication may be reproduced, stored in a retrieval system, or transmitted in any form by any means, electronic, mechanical, photocopying, or otherwise, without the prior written permission of the publisher, Triumph Books LLC, 814 North Franklin Street, Chicago, Illinois 60610.

Library of Congress Cataloging-in-Publication Data available upon request.

This book is available in quantity at special discounts for your group or organization. For further information, contact:

Triumph Books LLC
814 North Franklin Street
Chicago, Illinois 60610
(312) 337-0747
www.triumphbooks.com

Printed in U.S.A.
ISBN: 978-1-63727-947-2
Editorial production and design by Alex Lubertozzi
Cover and Teammate Spotlight illustrations by Giulio Pappalardo

All exercises, drills, and other instructional content contained within this book are for educational use only. This content is not intended to be a substitute for professional medical advice, diagnosis, or treatment. Always seek the advice of your physician or other qualified health provider with any questions you may have before taking part in any exercise program. The author and publisher disclaim any responsibility for liability, loss, or risk, personal or otherwise, which is incurred as a consequence, directly or indirectly, of the use or application of the contents of this book.

Contents

Foreword by Vanita Krouch ix

Intro: The Super Bowl Commercial Heard 'Round the World 3

1. Anyone Can Play 9
    Are you ready for some flag football?
    Shortened **FLAG FOOTBALL RULES** in my own words

2. Get Mental 19
    How US National Team player **ASHLEA KLAM** wins the
        mental game
    My interview with **DIANA FLORES** and the words that empower
    Getting in flow state like actor **MATTHEW McCONAUGHEY**

3. Team Bonding 33
    How **MARSHAWN "BEAST MODE" LYNCH** bonded his team
        over a bag of Skittles
    Multi-sport pro athlete **JOSH BOOTY** on the two ways a team
        can bond
    TEAMMATE SPOTLIGHT: Know your team
    TEAMMATE SPOTLIGHT: Bring the energy

4. Look Good, Feel Good, Play Good 43
    Colorado coach **DEION SANDERS** teaches us how looking good, feeling good, and having confidence can change your game dramatically

    How Nike's **DRIPPY UNIFORMS** changed the University of Oregon's brand forever

5. Do Your Job. 51
    When your Turkey Day family football game gets cray

    How the **PATRIOTS MOTTO** can help you become a powerhouse team

    Grab your broomsticks: **QUIDDITCH** is a real sport!

    PATRICK MAHOMES' viral left-handed throw—nailing every part of your job

    TEAMMATE SPOTLIGHT: Play like no one's on you

    Trick plays take practice! Let's talk about **"THE PHILLY SPECIAL"**

6. Ready to Rumble. 59
    How Detroit Lions receiver **AMON-RA ST. BROWN** got Velcro hands

    My Interview with Super Bowl champ **ANDREW WHITWORTH** on playing many sports

    DRILLS to help with catching, speed, and being ready to receive

    That time when Chiefs tight end **TRAVIS KELCE** wanted it so bad

7. Offense—Learn from the Pros 71

    How Detroit Lions quarterback Jared Goff pranked some college students

    My interview with **JARED GOFF**—inside tips for quarterbacks and flag football players

    Pro Trainer **EXERCISES** and skill games for all offensive positions

    TEAMMATE SPOTLIGHT: Shake and bake

    TIPS for quarterbacks, centers, and receivers

8. Hips Don't Lie—Defense 87

    Defense's greatest **CINDERELLA STORY**

    TIPS for defenders and rushers

    Pro Trainer **EXERCISES** and skill games for all defensive positions

    TEAMMATE SPOTLIGHT: The rush queen

    UNIVERSAL MOVEMENTS for all flag football players

    TEAMMATE SPOTLIGHT: The flag-pulling machine

9. Get Prepped 99

    My interview with NFL Hall of Famer and Good Morning America host **MICHAEL STRAHAN**

    TIPS for managing your time, sleep, and habits

10. It Ain't Over 'til It's Over 115

    TOM BRADY is the king of comebacks

    TEAMMATE SPOTLIGHT: Tears don't mean it's over

    My interview with LA Rams quarterback **MATTHEW STAFFORD** on the character needed to make a comeback

11. **The Future of Flag** 123
   *The **TAYLOR SWIFT** effect*
   Spreading the game
   *My fireside chat with FOX Sports' **JOEL KLATT** on college and Olympics*
   *My interview with **IZELL REESE**, director of NFL Flag, on the future of flag*

About the Author. 131

FOREWORD
by Vanita Krouch

When AnnaSofia and I finally got on the phone, after playing phone tag and juggling different time zones, I was in Mexico on a US Embassy Sports Envoy trip working with youth athletes, and we were both preparing to compete in the 2025 US Select Bowl tournament in Los Angeles. I soon discovered that this young woman isn't just playing the sport at the top levels, she's growing the game worldwide. Girls are showing up in record numbers from every other sport to play flag football all while flag is headed to the Olympics. And now, finally, there's a book that speaks to us, for us, and from us.

    I grew up playing lots of sports—soccer, track, volleyball, softball, and basketball—and ultimately earned a D-1 basketball scholarship to SMU. But when I found flag, something new came alive inside of me. It was the most fun and addictive sport I had ever experienced! There's a uniqueness, a creativity, and an explosiveness to the game. I signed up for nine—yes, nine!—leagues so I could play in a game almost every night of the week. Any representation I had ever seen up until that point was boys playing the sport, so there was something empowering about beating the guys at their own game.

As the quarterback of the US Women's National Flag Football Team, there is no bigger honor than playing for the red, white, and blue. The sisterhood I share with my teammates is like nothing else. Flag has opened doors I could never have imagined, like participating in two Super Bowl commercials, coaching an NFL Pro Bowl team, and traveling to Finland, Israel, Canada, Germany, Mexico, and Panama. I am seeing firsthand how this sport has caught on like wildfire. And this book? It's showing up right on time.

So whether you're new to the sport or already calling plays, this guide is for you. Use it, tell your friends about it, then go light up the field. Because we're not just growing the game anymore. We're owning it!

—Vanita Krouch

June 2025

We Run This House

INTRO

The Super Bowl Commercial Heard 'Round the World

It's February 2023: Super Bowl LVIII. I'm at home in California with my family, just about to snatch a few nachos during a commercial break. I don't know it yet, but history is about to be made.

Diana Flores, captain of the world-champion Mexican Women's Flag Football National Team, stars in an ad made by the NFL. It opens up in the stadium, where everyone from sideline reporters to the arena staff to famous male football players are trying to grab her flags. Diana uses some sick moves to dodge them—and I recognize these guys! Cam Heyward of the Pittsburgh Steelers and Jalen Ramsey of the LA Rams! Diana gets chased out of the stadium and keeps running, leaping through a mall and parkour-ing her way to her home, where even her mom is in on the joke. It seems like everyone in the world wants a swipe at her yellow flags.

Standing there, I'm thinking, "Wait a minute...that's *my* sport!"

What happened that day on TV was historic because it showed that the NFL was getting behind something new, and something for girls like me. "Alexa" told me that a Super Bowl ad costs about $8 million for 30 seconds. So the NFL must have really wanted to share how pumped they were about women's flag football. The ad ended on the coolest note: "To the women pushing football forward, we can't wait to see where you take this game." This was big.

I got that same feeling something big was happening earlier that year. My girls flag travel team, the OC Seals, won the California/Nevada LA Rams Regional Tournament to represent California and Nevada in our first NFL Flag National Championship in Las Vegas. The moment we stepped onto those playing fields, the people hosting the event and the brand sponsors treated us like real pro athletes. Swag bag? Check. Free Subway sandwiches for lunch? Check. And the best part was, after playing against boys for so many years, we were surrounded by hundreds of girls from all over the country who love this sport just like we do.

It's been a big few years for Females in Flag, a movement backed by the NFL, promoting the growth of the game. In 2021, women's flag football became an NAIA college sport, and in 2024 it became an official high school sport. Division I colleges are getting on board too! And the biggest news is that flag football for both men and women has been announced as an official 2028 Olympic sport. Wow. America's favorite sport just opened the gates for women!

As a 14-year-old singer-songwriter and flag football player, I was so inspired that I decided to write a song with the crazy dream of it becoming the theme song for Females in Flag. I wanted to bring more girls into the sport I love, and I also wanted a fun hype song to get women pumped up to play. Being part of history is a pretty big deal! After writing the song, I worked with music producer Ike Nichols and recorded the vocal track at Paramount Recording Studios. Paying to record a song took a *lot* of babysitting hours, so I racked my brain about how to reach someone at the NFL to really blow the song up. Luckily, we have a family friend, Kaylee Hartung, a reporter for the *Today* show and Amazon Prime football. I sent her my song, "We Run This House," and she shared it that same day with Jane Skinner, the NFL commissioner's wife! I learned that Jane

Skinner was a leader in the Females in Flag movement. Within a week, everyone at the NFL offices in New York City had heard the song.

Flash forward to the 2024 NFL Pro Bowl, and I'm standing on the field being interviewed by NFL Network's MJ Acosta-Ruiz as my song, "We Run This House," plays for 54,000 people, celebrating all these amazing girls in the game. I couldn't believe it. Instead of watching her on TV, I actually stood next to Diana Flores from the Mexican national team and talked with her about how far the game had come since we were playing against boys in our hometowns.

This book is going to give you an intro to girls flag football and some insights that will help you up your game. I'm not an expert or coach or even the best on my team, so why am I qualified to write this? Well, I was lucky enough to be born in the right place and the right time. In my hometown, Newport Beach, flag football is a big deal. Former USC and NFL quarterback, and now college football commentator Matt Leinart had the vision to start a flag league right in my backyard. The league has grown to 12,000 players in eight cities. I started in this league when there was no one to play with or against other than boys. I played on my big brother's team—thanks to him for being chill with it!—starting at the age of eight until there were enough players to eventually form girls teams.

But where I really hit the jackpot is that the dad of one of my best friends has been our coach since we were little. Jason Guyser is the coach of the current No. 1 high school flag football team in the country, Newport Harbor High School. Coach Guyser coaches our travel team, the OC Seals, which has competed three years in the NFL Flag Championships at the Pro Bowl. At the time I'm writing this, we are ranked No. 1 by USA Football. Coach Guyser is a huge role model for me and has revolutionized how I understand and play the game. His name has become well known in the flag football world. He's always been there for me and has truly changed my life.

I'm not the star of my team—you'll learn about some of my awesome teammates in this book—but I can tell you that I've been fortunate enough to play with some of the most talented players in the country and learn from an incredible coach. My journey of playing this very young sport in its most exciting time and playing with some of the best has taught me some really amazing lessons and tips that I can now share with you!

CHAPTER 1.
Anyone Can Play

flag football girl / *noun*
1 : same as a normal girl, just much cooler

So many people give up on things they want to do because they think it takes too much time to learn and master them. But flag football is a sport that anyone can play, starting today! One of the coolest things about flag is learning from scratch and then making plays happen with your friends. Don't have friends who play? Ask them to learn with you. I grew up with an amazing group of girls who were willing to learn the game and just have fun with the process together. The secret about flag football? It's only as fun as you make it. So get everyone you know and just start playing!

Sure, tackle football is cool, but it can be hard to learn because of the advanced tackling techniques and plays. There are pads and equipment involved. But in flag football, the format is way more simple. You only need cleats, a ball, and flags. The basics are catching, throwing, and running. You can practice by just throwing and catching with each other and learning simple routes. If there isn't a local team, it's all good—you can make one! You might be surprised to know that it only takes five girls. Flag football is easy to learn because all you've got to know is your route and your job. So why not give it a shot? You'll have the time of your life, and you'll even wonder why you didn't start sooner.

This book is meant for a range of players, from young beginners to older, more experienced players hoping to get to the D-1 college level, so hear me out for a minute as I break down the game. If you already know the ins and outs, this book is like a "choose your own adventure"—just skip ahead to the parts that apply to *you*.

THE BASICS
(Football without the Visits to the ER)

All right, so flag football is less violent than tackle football, but it's just as intense and exciting. There's no tackling, no body slams, no flying elbows—just pure athleticism, strategy, and skill. You're pulling flags off belts instead of smashing people to the ground like you're Dwayne "The Rock" Johnson in his former WWE wrestling career. Flag is way more civilized but just as heart-pounding. In flag football there are so many opportunities for creativity and massive plays! Also, unlike tackle football, where some guys never even touch a ball, in flag almost everyone on the field has an opportunity, even on defense. Just as in tackle football, everyone on the field has an important role. But the game is less about physicality and more about finesse.

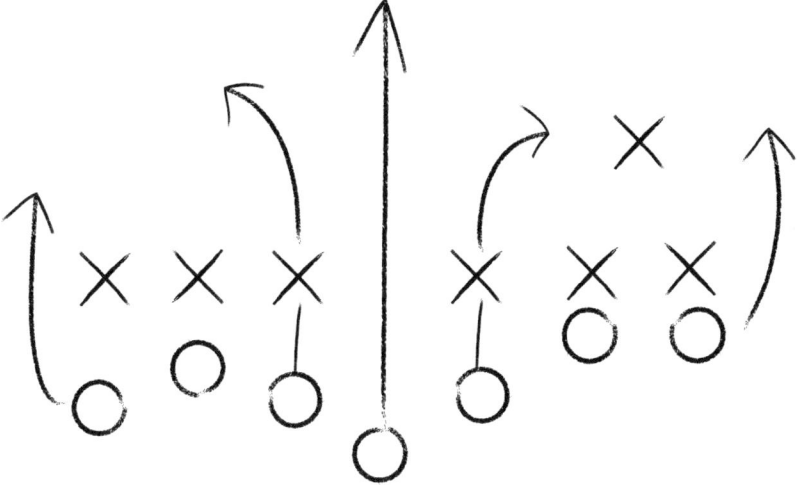

Team Size

It's usually five to seven players per side, depending on the league. What's the difference? Well, fewer players means more field space and more room for epic plays. The thing about having fewer players is that it's more important when you are on defense. If you let a player get behind you, then you have fewer teammates to help out. It becomes a big speed game. When there are more players, the game immediately becomes more aggressive because you have to fight against more players in a small space to catch the ball. Either way, it's always good to be aggressive and fast when you're playing.

The Field

Sometimes we play on full-sized football fields, and sometimes we play on fields just a fraction of that size. Imagine a football field but shrunken down, like a snack-sized bag of Doritos. Those smaller fields are about 60–80 yards long and 20–30 yards wide, with end zones at both ends.

Winning (What We Came For)

The mission? Get the football into the end zone as many times as humanly possible, especially since you have a limited number of series (possessions). A touchdown is worth six points and extra points are worth one or two points. Rack 'em up!

How to Play

KICKOFF (BUT NOT REALLY)

Forget the giant kickoff that starts regular football games—this is flag football. At the beginning of the game, the refs start the offense somewhere between the 5- and 20-yard line, depending on the size of the field. It's kind of like starting a Mario Kart race at the back of the pack—you've got to work your way up.

FOUR DOWNS TO FINISH

You've got four tries (downs) to move the ball 10 yards from where you started. If you make it, congrats! You get another four downs. If not, the other team takes over, and it's time to lock in on defense.

RUNNING VS. PASSING

At the start of every play, the center snaps the ball to the quarterback (QB), who decides whether they want to pass the ball or run it. Depending on the rules, there are limited times that the QB can run per game, quarter, series, etc.

THE FLAG PULL

Instead of tackling, players snatch the flag from your belt. If your flag gets pulled, you're "down" right there. Or, if you have the ball and the ball hits the ground, it's also "down." If the ball ever touches the ground during a play, the play is dead—there are no "fumbles." Likewise, if your body hits the ground, you're down. The only parts of your body that can touch the field while you have the ball and keep the play alive are your hands and feet. The floor is lava for any other body part—elbows, knees, etc. Even if your flags are still intact, the play is over.

Scoring

TOUCHDOWN

Six points is all you need! Run it in, catch it in the end zone, whatever you do, it is all valid. You only have so much time to score and have possession so make sure you're racking up those points! Even if you are on defense, if you intercept the ball and go in your end zone you can still score a touchdown.

EXTRA POINTS

After a touchdown, you get one shot at some more points:

- One point if you start from the 5-yard line.
- Two points if you start from the 10-yard line (if you are willing to take those risks).

No field goals, no problem—just pure confidence. Personally, I think field goals would be pretty fun to add because so many girls around the world that play flag football also play soccer, but for now, we are all about running, throwing, and receiving to score points.

Positions

QUARTERBACK

QBs are mainly in charge and make most of the decisions on whom to throw to. They're throwing passes, handing off the ball, and praying their teammates catch it.

RECEIVERS

Their job is to catch the ball and look good doing it. They catch all the balls and make sure they get as many yards as they can.

RUNNING BACK

The track star. They take the ball and haul down the field like their life depends on it.

DEFENDERS

The game-changers. They're out there pulling flags to make sure the play stops as quickly as possible. They can intercept the ball, too, and shift the game's momentum.

Penalties

Look, you can't just do whatever you want. Break the rules, and you'll get flagged (penalized, not the other kind of flag). Sometimes there are things you can do to make the other team get a penalty, but usually you want to avoid one against you. Fouls include:

OFFSIDE

Jumping the gun before the ball's snapped.

HOLDING

Restraining a player who doesn't have the ball.

FLAG GUARDING

Swatting someone's hand away while they're trying to snag your flag. What you want to do instead is to move the rest of your body in different ways to make the flag as unreachable as possible.

PASS INTERFERENCE

You cannot swat someone's hand away or clobber them as they are reaching up for a ball. What you can do is knock the ball down or try to catch it yourself because you have every right to catch that ball just like the offense. So there is no foul if you are just trying to get the ball. Penalties usually cost you yards, so the moral of the story? Play fair, or the refs will humble you real quick.

Strategy

FAKE PLAYS

Nothing's more entertaining than watching the defense scramble because you faked a throw and ran it yourself. There are many plays you can do as a trick play. They are not only fun to do but also fun to watch from the stands.

SPEED IS EVERYTHING

Fast runners are clutch in this game. If you are fast, it's easy to beat defenders and it's easier to guard your man when you are on defense.

GET LOUD

Get as loud as you can when you call out plays, and yell when someone's open. On defense, it is good to communicate about who is guarding whom.

WRAPPING IT UP

Women's flag football is all about speed, skill, and pulling off crazy plays that make people go, "No way she just did that!" It's like regular football, but at a faster pace without the tackling. So there you have it.

If you are starting flag football for the very first time, or you're looking to take your game to the next level, there are great inspirational stories all around us. The Philippines started their own national flag football team in 2023 and went on to win a game at the IFAF Women's Asia Oceania Flag Football Championship that same year! The team was full of girls who were completely new to flag football, but they set their minds on a common goal and trained like crazy. Now one of the team members who is new to the sport, Bea Ignacio, has become an ambassador for flag football and is helping to grow the game in her country. Remember, every experienced player was once a beginner, and some were beginners not long ago!

Now let's get into the good stuff, the secret sauce, the tricks and tools I've learned from my coach and some of the best minds and players in the NFL!

CHAPTER 2.
Get Mental

IN YOUR HEAD

Here's something I've learned from my own experience as a receiver. When I'm not playing well and not catching balls, it's not always my physical technique—it's sometimes that I am getting stuck in my own head. "What if I miss this? What if my defender gets her hands on it? This is our last chance to get a first down!" Overthinking and feeling pressure to catch a ball can cause me to drop it. I have started to train myself to just lock in, while still having the correct technique. What that means is that I use my instincts and just react to the ball, because I spend lots of practice time working on the right technique.

IN THE ZONE

When you are present in the moment, you find your "flow state," which means being in the zone, or locked in. That's when you perform your best! You know how Spider-Man is able to slow down his sense of time to dodge a bullet or a punch? The Spider-Man 2 video game allows players to slow down time to 70, 50, or even 30 percent of normal time to fight bad guys. Getting into flow state kind of lets you do that. It's a term used in positive psychology to describe how the brain experiences time differently and performs better when you're just focusing on your task and not judging what's happening at the same time. You just do it, not thinking about the fact that you're doing it. Sound familiar, Nike?

MENTALITY WITH ASHLEA KLAM

I had a chance to sit down and talk with Ashlea Klam, one of the youngest members on the US Women's Flag Football National Team. I caught her between her college classes at Keiser University in Florida and her daily football practice, and you might have seen her in the recent Super Bowl LIX commercial! From the age of seven, Ashlea competed against the boys, and because there were no flag football teams for girls in the area, her parents had to start their own team. They named it "Texas Fury" with the dream of it becoming a contender nationally, and it's now a massive and successful club in three Texas cities.

ASHLEA KLAM

You can watch the entire interview on @annasofiadickens on YouTube, but here are some really cool insights and stories from Ashlea. Throughout Ashlea's football journey, she learned a lot about the mental side of the game:

"I never really understood that there are two sides to football. You have your physical skill level and you have your mentality and your mental skill level. I never realized that until

I got to the age where my mentality was tested. When I got to that age, I realized, okay, I need to work on this as well. So I always tell younger girls that good athletes make mistakes and great athletes make mistakes. But what makes them great is how they react to them." Ashlea explained that when she makes a mistake, she asks herself three questions:

Ashlea's 3 Questions
1. What could I have done to avoid that?
2. What can I do to fix it right now?
3. What can I do to make sure it doesn't happen again?

Ashlea: I remember I was in the France game where I was wide open and I dropped a corner post. In my mind, I could have easily been like, "I'm terrible, I shouldn't be here, I don't deserve to be here." I could have easily broken myself down. And that would have been the end of that. I wouldn't have been able to get back up to where I was playing and that could have been it. But instead I thought, "Okay, what was one thing that I did that made me make that mistake?" I looked too soon at the ground to see where I was. And you know this, if you're doing a corner, you need to make sure that you [have] the IQ of field awareness.... So I looked too early and I ended up just losing concentration on the ball.

So two, what can I do to fix that? What could I have done to avoid that mistake? I could have made my corner a little bit longer so that I wasn't so close to the sideline.

Then three, what can I do next time to avoid that mistake? And it's basically knowing what you're gonna do right before the snap. So that's something that's always helped me. It's just kind of evaluating what I could have done instead of bringing myself down. And that's something that definitely really helped me.

I also had a huge drop in the Mexico game at the IFAF Continentals Cup. And at that moment, I shut down. I let it break me down and I was in my head the entire time. I even took myself out of the play, which I shouldn't have done. I should have had the confidence in myself that I was gonna make that up. But I shut down, and we ended up going to second down. I took myself out. Someone else went to center. Vanita [Krouch, the QB of the US National Team] was 15 yards back. They haven't practiced her being 15 yards back, so it was a lower snap, and the play didn't end up working out. So now it's third down, and we needed to score that drive. So I went to the sideline and I thought of things that I could do and I went back out there. Then my coach called the exact same play, literally the exact same play and I freaked out. I was like, "My gosh, he has so much trust in me right now. He has trust in me, so does my quarterback, and I need to have trust in myself." So then I went back out, made the play, and we ended up scoring on that drive [to win the world championship game!].

So there really are two things that you can choose. You can either let it take away all of the work that you have done to get to that point, or you can grow from it. I definitely took the approach of growing from it, which helped me tremendously.

Hearing that from Ashlea is really inspiring because it expands on the mental part of the game. As she was saying, it's all about what you choose to do with your mistakes. It differentiates people and really shows who you are based on your reactions to things. Checking yourself and learning and growing also means you have potential to be really coachable. To be coachable means that you take constructive criticism—tough advice that actually makes you better—and apply advice you have received to your game. Being coachable is a quality you want to have if you want to get better and constantly improve yourself. And it's no surprise that being coachable can be the No. 1 quality coaches look for! If your mind is open to change, then there's room to grow as a player.

DIANA FLORES

TALKING WITH Diana Flores, quarterback of the Mexican Women's Flag Football National Team, I learned so much about how we can't control outside forces and stereotypes, but we can control our own mental strength and set our own personal goals. You can watch the entire interview on @annasofiadickens on YouTube, but here is some of our conversation:

AnnaSofia: We both talked about how we also grew up playing with boys because there weren't many girls to play with. What was that like?

Diana: It was an amazing experience.... At the beginning, I won't lie, it was a challenge because until that time that I started playing with boys, it was the first time I played with boys my age. I was the only girl in the league. And it was challenging because it was the first time I got to see for myself and experience all these mental barriers or misconceptions about what a girl can or cannot do, you know, stereotypes. I saw them. I mean, I did before, but this time it was next to me. And at the beginning, it was hard because I couldn't understand why. I remember going to every practice and asking myself, "Why are they not taking me seriously? Why are they underestimating me if they've seen what I can do, if they've seen that I'm good at this?—and I'm not only good, I'm better than many of my teammates here. So I couldn't understand why.

But I think it was very important that my parents were in every step of the way and never let me give up. Because in that way I understood, and this is one of the biggest lessons I have had, that sometimes the way people react in this scenario, my teammates, it's not against you. It's nothing personal to you. It's sadly maybe the way they grew up, sadly maybe the way the culture is built around all these stereotypes or the gender barriers. But it has nothing to do with you personally. So don't take anything personally. And instead of fighting against that, help them to connect with you, help them to understand that you are there to build something better and bigger and that you have the same passion and love that they do for the game. That was the most important thing for me.

Once I understood that, everything changed, things just started to be good. I started playing more days. They could see that I had this drive to be the best on the field and do the best thing for the team, and I could see how their mentality completely changed. Now they were the ones backing me up against other teams, all their boys. Now they were like true teammates. And I think that's the power of sport. And I love to see how sport keeps breaking barriers in every scenario.

AnnaSofia: That's so inspiring, and of course I feel like I went through the exact same thing. I had to play on my older brother's team and my dad was the coach, and all these older boys were like, "What is she doing here? It's just 'cause her dad's the coach." I'm like, "No, it's because there were no other girls that I could play with." And I wanted to show them that I was good at the sport, too. I wanted to show my brother that I could play. And having to earn all of the boys' respect and to show that I could have a spot on the team was a really hard thing. But I ended up learning so much from that, and it was such a great experience. I remember one time I was playing with my older brother and I had this one chance to catch a touchdown pass to score my first touchdown, but my brother caught the pass that was headed to me. I was so down and I just remember I was like, "You know what, from now on I'm going to make sure I get my chances." So playing with the boys was a really memorable experience.

It sounds like you had a great relationship with your dad. How did he help you get into the sport?

Diana: He was the one who introduced me to this amazing world of football and flag football. Before getting to know the sport, I used to do other activities like ballet, gymnastics, jazz. My mom was a dancer, so I think she kind of wanted me to go through that path. But it wasn't my thing. I remember I was in the ballet classes, like being the only girl trying to persuade all the girls to play games before the class and run around the classroom, because that was my thing. And so one day my dad came home and took me to a football field to watch a flag football practice. We went to watch these women play flag. And I didn't know anything about the game, anything about the sport, never seen it on TV before. But just to see all these women being themselves there, not being judged by anyone, just being rude, all that passion on the field, running on the field, throwing the ball, all that power. I think that's what made me fall in love that very first time with the game. And the day after, I was there training. So I was super lucky that that coach at that time let me be part of the team, even if I was the youngest girl there. But I think maybe he could see, you know, I don't know, like my passion and how happy I was just to be there. So he gave me a chance, and ever since then, I haven't been able to [leave].

AnnaSofia: That's so relatable because I used to do competition dance as well, and I was like, "Dance is my thing." I thought I was going to be a dancer for the rest of my life, and I was doing so many dance classes a day, but I was also the one in class just looking forward to the strength competitions where you had to hold a pose for the longest. And I realized I like competition. I like athleticism. I like playing games. I don't like dancing on a stage. So that's when I transitioned from dance to football.

Diana: That's amazing.

AnnaSofia: It was so cool to hear how your dad brought you to the game of flag football. What are some of the most important things that your dad has taught you?

Diana: I think the most important thing my dad cultivated in me, not only my dad, my mom too, is to connect with my inner power. They used to tell me since I was very, very young—and this was our thing—they used to tell me always, "Remember you're powerful. You are powerful. You are powerful." Almost every day before going to bed, "You're powerful." So it became like a normal thing for me to listen to that. And I kind of, through time, just owned it. But as I grew up, I realized that it is not a common thing that parents tell those kinds of encouraging words to their kids. And it is not a normal thing that most of us are able to recognize and embrace our own power. And what I mean with power is just embracing who you are, all your strengths, or your opportunity areas. So I believe that has been the biggest lesson that has guided me through every challenge in life, not only in my career as an athlete but also as a woman, also as a professional in every area.

AnnaSofia: Yeah, and that's a really important thing to be told, especially as a young teenage athlete. I mean, you were told you weren't tall enough, strong enough to play quarterback for so many years. How did it feel to prove them all wrong?

Diana: I think for me, the main focus was not to prove everybody else wrong, it was to prove to myself that I was what I believed in my mind I could be. So since I was very, very young, I feel somehow that has been my mindset, or my main focus, to prove to myself that the vision I have in my head [of myself], it's me.

Diana Flores is a great example of someone who let a simple message guide her—"I am powerful." You want to be careful not to get too stuck in your own head. I once heard actor and author Matthew McConaughey say that you don't want to be under the moment looking up at it because it feels big, or above the moment looking down on it because it feels small. Instead, you want to be right in the moment. This is something I'm working on every day.

DON'T LET THE MOMENT FEEL TOO SMALL

When you let the moment feel too small, you could be thinking that this game doesn't matter. You might be thinking that this game or this practice is no big deal. But every game, practice, and rep matters if you want to get better. Even if it's just a scrimmage or a practice, you can't minimize it.

This reminds me of something pretty unforgettable that Deion Sanders said. Sanders, who earned the nickname "Prime Time," was an electric player on the field. He was the only athlete in history to compete in both a Super Bowl and a World Series. Sanders said, "My top plays happened in practice when no one was looking." Every practice mattered, and no moment was too small.

DON'T LET THE MOMENT FEEL TOO BIG

On the other hand, if you let the moment you're in feel too big, like this game is all or nothing, it keeps you from staying in the moment and doing your best. So, when you want to make sure a game time moment doesn't feel too big or overwhelming, practice and preparation helps you lock in to what you are doing. You're looking for a chance to make a difference in the game. Tell yourself in the moment that just one small thing like a catch could get your team a win, touchdown, or even a first down. Every little thing matters, and it's important to remind yourself of that every moment of the game. When I am playing, I talk to myself constantly before each play so I know and understand my assignment. It makes me more focused and it makes me remember the little things when the play starts. It is almost like scanning through terms before a test to keep things fresh in your mind.

MOTOR IMAGERY IS THE REAL DEAL

Mental preparation plays a bigger part than you might think. Even if you are just running through things in your head, it translates to your muscles. Just like if you are learning a dance, if you are "marking" it in your head (running it through in your mind), it leads you to do the dance better "full out" when it's time. Running through things in your head works almost as much as doing the actual motions. It's called "motor imagery," meaning that you are imagining moving. You are using almost the same neuron pathways—the paths that your brain's electrical signals shoot through—when you think about something as when you physically do it. Like if you watch a video of yourself doing something and then you visualize how to do it better, it actually helps you do it better! So apply this to everything you do. Really visualize yourself running perfect routes, catching challenging balls, doing advanced footwork, using speed technique, and winning games! All these things can really affect what you do in real life, and I suggest that you use this technique when preparing for big events or even small practices.

YOUR WORDS MATTER

Another big thing is verbal preparation. There is so much science behind what you say. Saying negative things can lead to negative emotions. There was actually a study titled "Bad Is Stronger Than Good" by Roy F. Baumeister et al. in the *Review of General Psychology* (2001) that shows negative words evoke way stronger emotions than neutral or positive words, and negative words paint even stronger pictures in our brains. Screaming motivating words changes the molecular structure of your brain! Just like motor imagery, words you say out loud change the neuron pathways. Even if you say something jokingly that you think you don't mean, like, "I am gonna lose, I am gonna fail, I am so tired," all those words will trick your brain into actually believing that. So always encourage yourself and use positive and loving words because words can hurt, but words can also heal. Words can set you up for all kinds of success, whether it's right now in a scrimmage and taking a test, or it's your long-term goals and dreams. Everything you say matters.

CHAPTER 3.
Team Bonding

SKITTLES FOR THE WIN!

Seattle Seahawks player Marshawn Lynch, famously called "Beast Mode," was once caught on camera eating Skittles after scoring a touchdown. The commentators joked about it and the fans started buzzing. It turns out Marshawn's mom used to give him Skittles before games as a kid, calling them "power pellets." Marshawn's Skittle-eating became even more famous when he scored a 67-yard touchdown against the New Orleans Saints in the 2010 playoffs, which people called "Beast Quake." Fans were saying that the Skittles gave him supernatural abilities. And after that, teammates would shower Skittles on him and fans would toss them from the stands after touchdowns. Marshawn even formed a partnership with Mars, the company that makes Skittles, and Mars would donate to Marshawn's Fam 1st Foundation when he scored. The Seahawks team had so much fun with this ridiculous tradition that it became part of their entire team's culture. The tradition even carried on after Marshawn Lynch retired! Sometimes these tiny, funny rituals can bring a team together.

Bonding with your team goes a long way on the field. What I've observed is that when the stakes are high, teams that haven't created bonds off the field break down in high-pressure situations. They blame, they yell. The players get discouraged. Even when the going gets tough, on my team, we say something encouraging to each other between each play. When it goes well, we celebrate.

The old adage, "You can discover more about a person in an hour of play than in a year of conversation," still holds true. Keeping the play in our lives is so important to our bonding. It lets us challenge each other in a healthy way. Every time we go on a tournament trip, we try to visit a fun place like an amusement park together so we can all get scared about the rides together. If that's not in our budget, we all just gather in someone's hotel room. For teams that play locally, anything you do off the field can be great bonding. My soccer coach, Nacho, hosts a murder mystery game by a fire pit. He also built a gigantic baseball diamond out of Slip 'N Slide tarps and kiddie pools, and we spent the evening using our soccer skills together, screaming and wiping out in the soapy water. One time our soccer coach even took us paintballing and, weirdly enough, we bonded over all the black and blue bruises on our legs! Even going to the mall together creates some shared funny moments.

If you think about it, we're lucky that we often get to play with some of the same girls for more than one season and sometimes our whole childhood. It's way harder for NFL teams to bond. Did you know they sometimes have 30–50 percent of their team change from season to season? So the bonding starts over from scratch! Matthew Stafford, the Los Angeles Rams quarterback, told me how it takes time and effort for teams to bond. Back when he was on the Detroit Lions, he started a tradition of hosting a Halloween party that has carried on with his new team, the Rams. What were some of the best costumes? He said Jordan Whittington came as Captain Jack Sparrow and Dan Orlowski and his wife came as Zack Galifanakis's character "Alan" and the blonde baby from the movie *The Hangover*. His wife was stuck to him in a baby carrier the entire night! So, Matthew was saying that you can have plenty of serious conversations over meals when you're bonding as a team, but it's great to get people out of their comfort zones and find something to laugh about.

Sometimes team bonding can happen in a way you never expected. With my team, the OC Seals, our moms have formed their own little ritual. In clutch games, they bark like Seals. It's a really ugly sound, and my mom can't get it to sound anything like an actual seal. The refs and camera guys laugh. It's also highly annoying to the other parents and the other team, but it unites us as a team. Hearing our parents from the sidelines cheering for us in any sort of way always motivates us. It makes us feel so supported and always pumps us up to do our best in the next play! If our parents are going to put themselves out there by screaming like idiots, then we have to make a good play as well to meet the expectation! It's our thing.

When we played our first Showdown Series in Southern California, it was nighttime and really cold—well, cold for a California night. Our team consisted of mostly high school freshmen with two eighth graders, and we were playing against some tough competition. Many of the girls on the other teams were high school seniors. We looked over at our moms and dads, and they were bundled up, jumping around and cheering in front of portable space heaters. My teammate Skylie Cid was like, "If our parents are gonna stand out here in the cold for six hours, let's bring home the trophy!" We brought it home that night. It was absolutely freezing. It was 10:00 at night, we had school the next day, and no one wanted to be there shaking to the bone. But that is where we changed our mindset. We got all pumped and excited and got our parents into it too! We huddled up before the last game and started jumping around and being all energetic and singing. I know, it sounds funny, but that energy heated us up, woke us up, and made us win! So make sure you bring up the energy to also bring up the game.

I talked to Josh Booty, who, like superstars Deion Sanders and Bo Jackson, was one of the only athletes to play Major League Baseball and be drafted in the NFL. After playing at a high school powerhouse in Louisiana called Evangel Christian Academy, at LSU, and working his way up through the baseball minor leagues to the majors, he had great perspective on team bonding. He talked about the two ways bonding can happen—through fun and through suffering. After playing parts of three seasons in the MLB for the Florida Marlins, Josh returned to college and played quarterback under legendary coach Nick Saban at LSU. First of all, can you imagine playing a pro sport and living on your own as an adult and then going back to college, going to class, and being a kid again? What a crazy transition. Not only do you have to sit through class, but you're also kind of the old guy who has to bond with his team really fast!

Nick Saban, not known for being the warmest, fuzziest guy, created a no-nonsense environment where, in an unusual way, the bonding could happen. Josh Booty said this: "[Coach Saban] comes in on the first day and he goes, 'Hey, we're going to win an SEC Championship and a national championship here. I just don't know if it's going to be with the guys in this room.' And so we were all like, 'Oh, okay!' 'So I'm about to start recruiting like y'all have never seen. So some of you guys are going to be here and some of you guys aren't going to be here at the end of the day. And the ones that are here are going to win.'" Hold on! Can you imagine your own coach saying that to your team? Like, "Someone's about to get voted off the island"? My teammates and I would be freaking out! Josh continued: "And so we're like, 'Whoa!' We paid attention really quick."

Nick Saban did what he said he would do. He went on to win a national championship for LSU three years later, and only some of those guys were along for the ride. But having a common feeling about your coach, whether your coach is scary or quirky or tough, can really bring a team closer together.

According to Josh Booty, tough training can also unite a team: "A big team-bonding experience is training together very hard. It's like the military or the SEALs, right? They train together. They go through these obstacles where you don't think you can make it. I was like, 'I can't drink Coke or eat Mexican food the day before I got to go work out for Saban's conditioning program.' And that was every day of the week! When you're in the trenches in the off-season working hard, going through different training cycles...that's the ultimate team bonding."

Bonding can happen all across the sport of flag football, not just within your own team.

When girls show good sportsmanship, it makes new players want to stick with the game and makes seasoned players

TEAMMATE SPOTLIGHT--KNOW YOUR TEAM

My team and I have been playing together our whole lives, and we are best friends on and off the field. When you watch us play, you can see the chemistry we have and the bonding behind every play. **SCARLETT GUYSER**, who is one of the best quarterbacks I know, has such a close bond with everyone on the field and knows us so well. This helps our game so much because she has a perfect sense of how fast each of us run, where we will probably end up, and many more things that require intuition. She has such a good eye for reading defenses and knows her teammates.

TEAM BONDING

feel that they are part of something bigger. Sometimes we play classy teams that tell us we did well, whether they won or lost. We played a team from Hawaii, Island Empire, who gave us custom team-name bracelets. I wear mine every day and will never forget that team. I'm not telling you this because you need to make bracelets. I'm saying that good sportsmanship is memorable and makes the sport even better. You are motivated to go out and practice and get drawn to a sport where you feel you are part of something bigger.

Not only do you want to have good sportsmanship toward your teammates and the opposing team, you also want to have good sportsmanship toward your coach. Jared Goff once told me that, if you have a problem with one of your coaches or how they do something, it is always good to have that respectable conversation with them rather than just letting that anger build up because they probably have something to talk to you about too. This way you can both improve and work it out, and a lot of coaches would appreciate having that conversation. Jared has had many different coaches while playing for Cal, the Rams, and the Lions.

WHAT YOU BRING TO THE FIELD

What type of attitude and mindset you bring to the field is very important. If you are having a bad day and everything seems to be falling apart, don't bring it on the field! Something I have learned is that if you bring negative energy into a game, it does not help at all. It forces you to seem mad and annoyed about

TEAMMATE SPOTLIGHT--BRING THE ENERGY

One of my best friends and favorite teammates, **ABBEY KROGH**, is such a great example of bringing the right energy to the field. No matter what mood I am in, she always makes me feel better. She is always in such a positive head space and brings so much laughter and energy to our team and to my life. Besides her amazing abilities as a rusher, this sometimes causes us to win the game because of her motivation right there beside us. Energy changes everything!

TEAM BONDING
41

everything. This can make you run slower or just take away your confidence, which could cost you the game. Another thing I have learned is that, if you have a problem with someone on your team, either resolve that problem or do not let it affect your game at all. It is always good to have some friendly competition, but when things go too far it could potentially split up a team. Instead, bring a positive and energetic mindset to the field. Carry your head high and have confidence in yourself.

CHAPTER 4.

Look Good, Feel Good, Play Good

Former NFL and MLB player Deion Sanders famously said, "If you look good, you feel good. If you feel good, you play good. If you play good, they pay good." This became Deion's mantra and is now a big part of the University of Colorado team that he coaches. Deion was way ahead of his time on the "tunnel fits" we see players doing today. The pro players show up to the game wearing their drippiest outfits. It's a way of saying, "Yeah, I'm ready. I came here to ball out." Now Deion isn't the only one who believes this mantra.

There are studies being done about this thing called "enclothed recognition." When I looked into it a little more, I realized it just means that clothes make you feel something. And having confidence can make you perform better. There's a Columbia Business School professor named Adam Galinsky who came to the conclusion that outfits actually do affect your performance ("Enclothed Cognition," *Journal of Experimental Social Psychology*, July 2012).

One of the best examples of enclothed recognition is the University of Oregon Ducks going from a mid-tier college football program with a no-name brand to a well-known powerhouse program. Back in the 1990s when my parents were in high school, if you talked about big football programs like Ohio State or Alabama and then mentioned Oregon, people would be like, "Who's that?" But then something changed. The University of Oregon happens to have a pretty cool alumnus named Phil Knight. This guy Phil ran track in college, and it's no coincidence that he worked with his track coach Bill Bowerman to start a company selling shoes to help people run fast. Just a couple hours from the University of Oregon is the headquarters of Phil Knight's company. In case you hadn't already guessed, the shoe company they started was Nike! So Nike started sponsoring Oregon's football program by revolutionizing the team uniforms. The Ducks, who had always had a traditional look, started taking the field with drippy, flashy, futuristic uniforms. It started with some thick, neon-yellow stripes, and led to different colors entirely, tire-track patterns, duck wings on the shoulders, and gold or shiny chrome helmets. They started changing it up from game to game, and it really caught people's attention.

WHAT'S YOUR BRAND?

The University of Oregon became known for creativity, disruption, and confidence. This was a major draw for new recruits. And with some upgraded facilities thanks to Nike, Oregon began attracting great football talent and began winning! Most importantly, Oregon had built a national brand. So what really is a brand, you might ask? A brand is different from your name and what you actually do. It's what people *think and feel* when they hear your name. For example, when I was a kid living in Los Angeles, there was no place to ride our bikes with all the steep hills. So we would head down to UCLA and ride bikes until some security guard would tell us, "No bikes in the quad!" and make us leave. UCLA is a university with great academics and sports. But when someone asked me as a kid, "What is UCLA?" I would say, "Riding bikes!" To me, that was what the brand "UCLA" meant. So what is your brand as a flag football player? Remember that team from Hawaii that gave us bracelets? I think of good sportsmanship when I think of them. What do people think and feel when they play against you and your teammates? What would your parents or your coach say *your* brand is?

Here are some things I'm working on to have a good personal brand as a player and teammate:

1. **Show Up on Time**—Be in charge of your practice and game times and make sure your parents know when you need to leave the house to get there on time. Sometimes I get ready without giving my mom a heads up on when we need to leave. I can't expect her to instantly jump up, take her splashing bowl of soup in the car, and find an instant babysitter for my little brother! Give your parents enough time to get ready to leave.
2. **Show Up Ready to Listen and Learn**—Sometimes I have a hard time with this one because I'm so excited to see my friends. We all go to different schools and want to catch up on what's going on socially. But I try to remember that this is our only chance to get better, and practice is short.
3. **Show Respect to the Coach**—Oftentimes, your football coaches will be parent volunteers. They give up their free time to teach you, so make it a great experience for them too. They are the most important part of your team, so make them feel that way.

So your brand can be your sportsmanship, your reliability, your respectfulness, and your style.

BLINGED UP FOR GAME TIME

Every tournament I go to, I see new teams with an even cooler style than the last. They're in glow mode! It is so cool to see all the different styles and colors from teams that all live in various parts of the country! Some teams have neon red tank tops and some teams have light blue from head to toe. Some have hair paint that matches their uniforms. A lot of tournaments I go to have a hair station where these professionals

will do your hair for free before the games start. They have all these colors and strings and beads to put in your braids, and it looks so cool! My team usually doesn't do it, because one of our teammates—thanks, Tessa!—will do all of our hair before the game. It looks just as good and also saves us time from waiting in those lines. We also put on some eye black for fun! This boosts our confidence and our performance because it feels more hype when we are all matching and stylish. Once, our little sisters got matching headbands, and their game was fire that night. You play better in style!

ACTIVATION MODE

As teen girls, we're not gonna go to games too blinged out. The most important part of Deion Sanders' motto is actually the "feel good" part. For my team, we rest up, we hydrate, we do our braids. Looking and feeling put-together to me is more like a symbol saying, "I got here early, I was ready for this, I took the time to braid my hair for this because this game matters to me." It's like having main character energy. This is your day and you came to play. Feeling ready makes you play harder and more focused.

How you look can even make an opponent play worse. A clinical psychologist named Jonathan Jenkins said that your appearance can intimidate opponents and affect their performance (USA Lacrosse Magazine). I've seen this myself when a team shows up all blinged up. They look like they showed up early, and that this is a game they care about.

Appearances can have a mental effect, but when you see a team looking fierce, don't let them fool you. Our team was often underestimated for our size and appearance at some of the national events where the other girls looked more intimidating. I've also played against girls who were tiny in size but fast as lightning. Show up ready to play your best game no matter what.

Looking good can also mean looking good athletically. Like, are you always playing like it's game time? If you go all-out in practice, you'll perform your best in games. We like to cheer for each other sometimes in practice like it's game time. When we do long balls, everyone on the team watches and cheers. It motivates me and my teammates to perform our best. And when we get out on the field to warm up before a game, we are focused and make sure to do it right. We run routes and catch balls with the same technique and precision we will use in the game.

CHAPTER 5.
Do Your Job

Picture this: it's Turkey Day and your whole extended family just gorged themselves on grandma's cooking. Someone yells, "Let's play football!" Touch football sounds like a fun idea, until you hit the grass and the chaos begins. The uncles argue over who's gonna be quarterback. The snap, which was terrible to begin with, gets intercepted by an uninvited neighbor's dog. Everyone scatters like there's an alien invasion. While your cousins are running routes that make zero sense, there's a kid you don't even recognize doing cartwheels across the field. The offense is a mess, and the defense is no better. Everyone is guarding the same person who they claim "looked open," and family members start to argue. You've got people trying to play every position at once, like your uncle trying to be receiver, referee, and coach at the same time. No one knows what the score is—grandma keeps asking and doesn't get an answer—but your team somehow still loses.

The thing I'm probably most thankful for on Thanksgiving is that flag football doesn't have to be as disorganized and chaotic as your family touch football game. On a flag football team, there are a variety of positions you can play, and you know your role every time. If everyone masters their position and does their job, it makes for a great and unified team! Especially if your special skills all work together. Sometimes you have to go with the flow and play whatever your coach wants you to. But sometimes specializing in one position and putting your main focus on one thing is better because you spend more time getting better at that one job, which could make you way stronger on the field. It's almost like growing up with all these different hobbies, but at some point you have to narrow it down so that you can put your time and energy into getting better at one thing. It is still always great to practice other positions too so that if the coach needs to move you around you are able to do so. But, if each player dedicates themselves to long and rigorous hours of practice for their position, it benefits the team and builds trust.

DO YOUR JOB

The former New England Patriots head coach Bill Belichick turned his motto, "Do Your Job," into a way of life for his team, which became the biggest football dynasty in history. Wide receiver Julian Edelman was a great example of the Do Your Job way of thinking. He came to the team after playing quarterback in college but had to switch positions completely and learn every position on special teams. He even had to practice tackling and holding, which couldn't be further from what he had done for most of his life. But Edelman showed such a willingness to get better at every task that he became an example of Patriot success. It's also important that each player brings their special skills to the team, and Edelman did just that. He was insanely good at shuttle drills and running laterally. Actually, he was so good that some of the coaches thought their laser-beam timer was broken, and they asked him to do the drills again! Edelman ended up bringing this lateral speed and ability to change directions quickly to the Patriots' offense. It was just what the team needed. As a receiver myself, I can see how those short routes are a must for getting first downs when it matters. I like to practice moving laterally like Edelman, because it's good for offense and defense.

EVERY JOB IS UNIQUE

In flag football, each position has a unique job, and everyone has to do it right to make plays work. If you haven't played flag yet, understanding the positions is key. It's kind of like the sport Quidditch in J.K. Rowling's Harry Potter books. Whether you're a chaser, a seeker, or a keeper really matters, and everyone has to collab midair on broomsticks to make it work. Did you know that Quidditch has become a *real* sport for Muggles? Yup! There are leagues in the US, UK, Australia, and Canada. It's an internationally recognized co-ed sport, now called "Quadball." The funniest part is you have to run with a plastic PVC pipe between your legs, pretending it's a broomstick! Anyway, my point is that flag football, just like every team sport, has special positions that make the bigger goal of winning possible.

We will break down the positions in the next chapters on offense and defense. But just know that they all have to work together to make the magic happen. Have you ever seen one of those Rube Goldberg machines? Goldberg was an American cartoonist who used to draw ridiculous contraptions that would perform one single task. There were so many moving parts that seemed unrelated, but each one led to the final task. For example, your phone vibrates, making a fidget spinner fall off the table, pulling on a wire, which tips a bottle, and the weight of the bottle turns the next page of this book for you. Well, with football, every little contribution to the play matters.

DO IT LIKE YOU MEAN IT

Every route matters. On offense, when you know the ball is coming your way, you focus extra hard to run a perfect route. But even if you aren't getting the ball thrown to you and you're just a decoy to draw the defender away, your job is important. So you should always run your route like you mean it! Fake out your defender like the whole world is watching. You can call for the ball, clap your hands, and run fast as if the ball was meant for you. This takes some good acting skills. I've seen fake hand-offs that had me fooled for at least a few seconds.

Don't get down if you are not the targeted route of the play, everyone on the field is important. Whatever your job is, do your best and have fun with it! A lot times, scouts or future coaches could be watching you. So play for them. A grandparent who came a long way to watch you play—play for them. Even a friend or sibling who took the time to come to your game, they are there to watch *you*! So play for them.

PERFECT EVERY PART OF YOUR JOB

Whatever position your coach puts you in, work on getting every part of your job dialed in. You never know when they'll come in handy! Kansas City Chiefs quarterback Patrick Mahomes shared in an ESPN broadcast that he practiced left-handed throws just in case he ever needed them in a real game situation. His extra work paid off when he threw a game-saving pass against the Denver Broncos. The pass went viral! Commentators said they couldn't believe Mahomes had mastered something so unconventional. Sometimes the dull work of sharpening skills can lead to a magical moment!

BE DEPENDABLE

It is very important that you are dependable for your team. This could mean you show up on time and put in as much or even more work than the rest of the team. It's also all about the extra work you put in. Legendary Lakers guard Kobe Bryant

TEAMMATE SPOTLIGHT-- PLAY LIKE NO ONE'S ON YOU

My teammate **TESSA RUSSELL** is a great example of someone who runs a solid route every time. She plays like none of the defenders are there! She runs her route in a game just like she does it in practice. She can juke and snatch the ball out of the air no matter who is on her. Her only focus is nailing her route and receiving the ball. She does her job. Tessa's skills were noticed by the USA Football Select coaches, and now she's doing those same moves to represent the USA!

once told his assistant coach, Phil Handy, that he didn't want to pass the ball to teammates who didn't have a good work ethic. Kobe was there long before and after practice perfecting his craft, but he didn't respect the guys who just showed up right before practice and left when it was over, doing the bare minimum.

As for us girls flag football players, we usually have to leave when practice is over because our parents are there to pick us up. But putting in extra work, whether it's running sprints, stretching our hips, or catching reps, extra practice can happen anytime and anywhere. Being dependable leads to getting targets and catching balls.

GETTING IT RIGHT MEANS MORE FUN

When everyone works together, there's more opportunity for fun. The Philadelphia Eagles had an iconic trick play called "The Philly Special," which actually worked in Super Bowl LII. Trick plays rarely make their way into game-time situations, but when they do, it's fire! The Eagles were leading the New England Patriots 15–12 with 38 seconds left in the first half. They were fourth-and-goal from the 1-yard line, but rather than just go for a field goal, the coach made a bold decision to go for a touchdown. Backup tight end Trey Burton threw a touchdown to quarterback Nick Foles. It took a ton of practice to get this trick play right, but it paid off, becoming one of the most iconic moments in NFL history.

CHAPTER 6.
Ready to Rumble

REPS REPS REPS

My dad always says, "You're not what you do, you're what you do every day." It has become my mantra! Nothing could be more true when it comes to getting good at catching the football, whether you play defense or offense. I saw an interview with Detroit Lions wide receiver Amon-Ra St. Brown where he said he catches 202 footballs every single day. My first thought was, "Um...why 202?" Well, St. Brown's dad once saw another player with great hands, and found out that the other player had bought a JUGS machine so he could catch 200 balls a day. St. Brown's dad was like, "Then we're gonna catch 202!"

I like that story because it shows that you've got to work a little harder than everyone else. 200 catches per day is already way more than most players. And just two more catches per day than your opponent who catches 200 adds up to 730 more catches per year.

A JUGS machine is a really expensive ball-shooting machine that NFL pros use. It will cost you thousands of dollars! But let's be real. What does it take for you and me to be great at catching the football? The answer is reps, reps, reps. Ask a

parent to throw you balls. If you can't get a parent, ask a little brother or sister to chuck balls at you. They don't need to throw you a perfect spiral. Any throw will do. In fact, the harder and more crazy they throw it at you, the better practice you get. Your brain gets used to catching every speed and angle. Just last night I saw an NFL quarterback do an under-pressure, shovel pass to a receiver. It was messy and the ball spun end over end, but my little seven-year-old brother said, "I could catch that!" because we practice catching those crazy balls that look more like punts than spirals. It helps us be ready for any kind of pass.

All that matters is you're getting reps. How many reps do you need? Only you can set that number. My question to you is this: can you carve out the time to catch 10 balls per day? Just 10 balls per day adds up to 3,650 catches per year!

Reps that make you better come in many forms and even through many sports. My mom was the high scorer on the Swedish National Women's Lacrosse Team. Her specialty was the "quick stick" shot at goal, like a quick catch-and-shoot. But it didn't come from thousands of catches and shots with a lacrosse stick, it was from doing short tennis volley drills

growing up with her dad when lacrosse wasn't even an option for girls in her hometown. She taught me that anything that builds your hand-eye coordination helps you catch footballs. Get those reps in, no matter what sport you're playing!

I interviewed Super Bowl–champion Andrew Whitworth of the LA Rams. Whit won the Walter Payton NFL Man of the Year award, and you can see him every Thursday night commentating on Amazon Prime football and also on his podcast *Fitz & Whit*. I bet you've seen him on GEICO commercials too! Whitworth told me that even with 16 NFL seasons—he was almost as old as Tom Brady when he retired!—one thing that means a lot to him is all the sports he played growing up. You can watch our whole interview on @annasofiadickens on YouTube. Here's some of our conversation:

AnnaSofia: I once heard you talking about how the best NFL players grew up playing multiple sports. How important is it to be a multi-sport athlete?

Whit: I think honestly it's one of the greatest things you can do as a young athlete because of numerous things, whether you're ever gonna play sports professionally. I think the task of learning new things, new traits, new challenges is really what helps develop you as a person. Because when you talk about sports or any kind of game…you're learning an athletic skill. So I don't know if we care if we're trying to hit a golf ball or we're trying to shoot a shot or throw a ball or catch a ball or jump over something, I'm learning a new skill set. And when I'm trying to learn that new skill set, there's gonna be challenges, there are things that I'm gonna have to overcome. There's gonna be coaching involved that I'm not gonna like sometimes. He's gonna tell me to do something in a different way. But all those things are gonna help me develop a character to not be afraid to challenge myself, to not be afraid to be challenged by other people, and to overcome. And I think whether you play sports in college or professionally, the ability to overcome challenges and to rise up and take on challenges and to just keep resetting the pieces and taking on those challenges are things that will pay off for you in life.

   I think basketball had a huge impact on me being able to move my feet and play offensive line and protect against defensive linemen rushing the quarterback.... Being a powerlifter in high school helped me have the strength to play offensive line in the NFL, and then baseball [helped with] hand-eye coordination, learning how to use my hands and put them where I wanted to go with those hand-eye coordination type things when I'm defending against people. All of those sports helped me be great professionally, but they also taught me a lot about learning how to control my body and to rise up to challenges.

AnnaSofia: Yeah, and I think the hand-eye coordination thing is a really big part of it too. Just playing all these sports that involve hand-eye coordination really carries on to other sports. When do you think an athlete should narrow it down to one sport?

Whit: I think life does that. I think inevitably, if you just keep taking on challenges and you keep on saying, "All right, I want to be great at things," I think life is going to probably put you in a place where eventually you're going to find this one sport that you're gonna go, "You know what, I'm at the point where this is the one that's the most important to me. It's the one I'm the most passionate about, and I'm ready to let go of the other ones." I think that you'll find that place and you'll find that peace like I did.

Okay, now that we've learned from Amon-Ra St. Brown about the importance of reps, and "Big Whit" on building skills through many sports, let's get busy with some tips for receiving the ball, or intercepting it if it's meant for someone else.

CATCHING TIME

Whether you play defense or offense, you're catching footballs. Here are the best tips I've learned on receiving:

1. **Diamonds:** Make a diamond with your hands by touching your thumbs and index fingers. When a ball comes at you up high, you reach up and catch the ball with your diamond. Creating a diamond keeps the ball from flying through your hands.
2. **Pinkies:** Now turn your palms up and cross your pinkie fingers. When a ball comes at you down low, if you can practice doing this, then the ball won't fly through your hands.
3. **Snatch**: Catch the ball like it's a newborn baby and don't let it bounce off your hands. Receive it with your fingers as you snatch it from the air. Then tuck the football into your shoulder with one hand.

SAY MY NAME

A fun drill that can help you practice catching from every angle is when you are standing with your back to a teammate or sibling/friend and they throw the ball at you and call your name. You only turn around when they call your name and you have to catch it quickly because the ball has already been thrown. The ball could be heading in any direction so you have to react fast!

UP YOUR SPEED

An important part of making catches is your speed. It depends on the route, but usually you need to run them as fast as you can. When running deep routes, it's important that you run them fast because you either need to outrun your defender and get the ball or draw the defenders back. Sometimes running your deep route fast is helpful for your teammates because you could be taking the defenders with you and creating space for your teammates doing short routes. This happens often when you're trying to gain a couple yards or get to a first down. Also, practice accelerating after you catch the ball and not just stopping. Sometimes, girls catch balls in practice, stop, and come back. But in a real game scenario, you would accelerate and keep running toward the end zone, so that's how my coach tells us to do it. You're building these habits in your brain so that you don't have to think of anything but the ball when it's game time. When I build habits, it makes it so much easier to focus because I am already naturally doing the right things. That is another reason why every rep counts, so you can build habits.

Wanna get faster? One thing you can do that's pretty simple is…sprint! It's surprising how many of us young players don't actually sprint several times per week. My teammates and I are lucky to have a soccer coach who makes us do suicides, but some flag football teams aren't practicing enough quick sprints.

WANT IT!

Good receivers *want* the ball. They are constantly looking for it, they are asking for it, they are creating space and calling for the ball so that the QB knows they are ready for it. Sometimes, you'll see the best receivers in the world pacing next to the coach on the sideline asking for reps. One famous example during Super Bowl LVIII was when Chiefs tight end Travis Kelce bumped into Coach Andy Reid and yelled in his face. It made headlines all over the world. Kelce admitted later that he took it too far and didn't mean to bump his coach or sound disrespectful, but he told the *Today* show that what he was trying to say was, "Just put me in, I'll score, I'll score." While there are lines you don't cross with your coaches, Coach Reid said later that he loves Travis Kelce's passion: "I love it, he's a competitor and I love it." And the players who want the opportunities and are hungry for them often get put in to show their skills.

READY TO RECEIVE

Here's how to know when to look for the ball when running a route. If you give eyes too early, you might not get where you need to be. The QB only has a few seconds to throw, depending on your league rules, so you'll need to be prepared to catch the ball right on the break of your route (right when you cut), whether it comes or not. And if there's no break in your route, don't wait too long to look for the ball.

PLAYMAKERS AND ENTERTAINERS

Being on offense means you are the playmakers. Offense is usually how you put points on the board. Being on defense means you're a game-breaker. You can shift the momentum of the entire game with one amazing play. Whatever your position, you should make plays like your life depends on it. As soon as you line up, get excited! People are there to see you and are just sitting on the edge of their seats praying for a cool play. So make sure when you line up you are ready and pumped. You can't forget that playing football is supposed to be fun! So make it fun every time you step foot on the line. It sounds simple, but tell yourself, "I am going to make a play." Personally, I get so motivated to wow the crowd because who wouldn't want to? So run every route like you mean it and get excited to make a play.

A big part of football is entertainment. That's why people watch! Yes, maybe your family comes to watch you. But there are so many people around the world looking for excitement and entertainment, so make that happen! Be the excitement and entertainer. If you do make a play, maybe do a celebration with your friends. It entertains the crowd and gets you fired up for the next play. When you look like you're having fun—smiling, joking, laughing, and playing your best—fans will enjoy watching way more. So give them something extra! Maybe add a little pep in your step when you're walking back to the line. It's easier said than done because you are focusing on the game, but try not to forget.

Let me tell you why having fun also affects how many points get scored. A guy named Liu Yang at Beijing Sport University did a study that showed that in loud environments, athletes who focus on motivation (why am I doing this and what makes me excited about this?) instead of skill (what exact technique should I use to succeed?) perform better. So, if you're motivated and having fun, you'll probably play better and win!

CHAPTER 7.
Offense—Learn from the Pros

In 2018, Jared Goff, quarterback for the Rams at the time, teamed up with Red Bull for a crazy prank. Jared is known for being cool and calm on the field. I mean, in September 2024 playing for the Detroit Lions, he threw a perfect game against the Seattle Seahawks, setting a record for completions without an incompletion, and he didn't even realize it. He was like, "Oh, I did that?" But even though he's very chill, Jared is actually really funny. Jared pulled up at Ventura College, a junior college in California, not as himself, but pretending to be a transfer with a fake persona—some random dude from somewhere named Dreaj Foge. That's kind of his last name backward—I see what you did there, Jared! He put on a ridiculous wig that looked like it was from a '70s sitcom, a fake neck tattoo and fake mole, and stepped on the field with this super awkward energy. The coach announced to the team that there was a new quarterback transfer, which made the current quarterbacks a little nervous. That is, they were nervous there would be some competition for their position, until they saw him make some terrible passes. He blamed it on random, unrelated things like, "See, sometimes the hair falls down on my right side, so the right side of the field is like, out for me." The other guys were probably thinking, "Has this guy ever played before?"

But then suddenly Dreaj Foge started throwing dimes. One straight into a guy's hands. The next one a deep bomb right on target! Was it a fluke? Nope, Jared started throwing lasers into every corner of the field and jaws dropped. The players and coaches were stunned: "Who *is* this guy?" When the big reveal happened, Jared took off the wig and the guys on the team went crazy!

This is a great story because there are only 32 starting NFL quarterbacks in the entire world. Their talent is way above the rest—you can't hide it with a wig or disguise it with a fake mole. It's undeniable! We need to watch what the pros do on TV to learn how to play our own game. And we're super lucky because I got to sit down with Jared Goff himself to give *We Run This House: The Girls' Guide to Flag Football* our own private advice session with one of the greatest QBs in the world! To watch the whole interview, go to annasofiadickens.com or @annasofiadickens on YouTube.

AnnaSofia: You've won so many prime-time games and played in a Super Bowl. How do you stay super calm and relaxed in big prime-time games?

JARED GOFF

Jared: Yeah, it's a good question. I guess I'm somewhat used to it now, but when I was younger and you know you're playing the big game, you try to do everything the same as you would in a regular game, I guess. I think putting a lot of pressure on yourself in practice, or maybe not on yourself, but when coaches are able to apply pressure to you in practice, a lot of the game situations become a little bit easier. So I guess making practice harder, pushing yourself in practice and making it a challenge definitely made the games easier.

OFFENSE--LEARN FROM THE PROS

AnnaSofia: For sure. And so much of the game is mental. So what do you think about and what do you not let yourself think about when you're playing the game? Like, what do you block out?

Jared: Yeah, you're blocking out all the noise, all the fans yelling at you and everyone booing you or whatever. And even sometimes you're blocking out [how] some of your coaches can get a little bit excited or too critical at times. And you sometimes have to block that out. And certainly at quarterback, you have to be even-keeled and be able to kind of remain that steady force that the team can look at throughout the whole game.

AnnaSofia: I talk in my book about the importance of team bonds. When you arrived in Detroit, how did you build trust with your offense? And specifically, how did you and Amon-Ra [St. Brown] become such a strong duo?

Jared: Yeah, great question. That's probably one of the bigger challenges when you're switching teams is getting comfortable with the guys and making sure they're comfortable with you. I wanted them to trust me as much as I needed to trust them. I needed to make sure they knew that they could trust me and just get to know them on a personal level. I think when you're friendly with guys and when you're friends with your teammates and you have an interest in them outside of football, guys tend to want to win for each other a little bit more.... So you want to create those bonds and become friends and learn about each other and learn about their families, where they're from and all that. And that was part of my work that off-season. And yeah, St. Brown was a part of that—he was a rookie—and getting to have him come in and work. And I think again, I go back to the same word: *trust*. He and I trust each other so much. He trusts where I'm gonna throw it. I trust where he's running. I trust him to go make the catch. He trusts that I'm not gonna throw him into a big hit. So, yeah, there's a whole lot of trust between him and me, and it's a whole lot of reps and practice that gets us there.

AnnaSofia: And I totally relate to that connection and trust that you need with your team and your quarterback, because one reason why my team and I do so well together is because we've grown up with the same quarterback, same receivers, just kind of the same team. We've been friends our whole lives, so that kind of trust and just knowing each other really does help you on the field, and I totally relate to that.

Jared: Right, right, and you care for each other.

AnnaSofia: Yeah, for sure. I mean, these are my best friends that I'm playing with, and even if I'm playing with a team that I don't know, I try to make sure that they become my best friends so we have that trust. Do you have any tips for the flag football quarterback when a rusher is closing in?

Jared: Yeah, you know, ironically, I just did the Pro Bowl, which is flag football. I was just doing that, and I don't have much experience with it otherwise. But, yeah, when the guy's closing in, I mean, I'm not fast enough, but if you are fast enough and you can make him...or her miss, that's, I think, your best option. Because that'll buy you the most time... if you can just make one quick move and scramble. Otherwise, just know where your quick routes are. I think that was something I was doing in the Pro Bowl was, if they wanted to blitz me, fine, I had to make sure I knew where my quickest option was so I could get rid of it. I'm not fast. I'm not faster than the guy blitzing me. So I don't have the luxury of running away from him. But if you do, then that's probably the better option.

AnnaSofia: Exactly. Do you think it'd give you more time to make a quick move and have the rusher have to come all the way back? Or should the quarterback kind of be focusing on her footwork and adjusting the throw?

Jared: I wouldn't focus on your footwork while you're playing. I think the footwork and all that's for practice. As soon as you get in the game, you just react. Let your body react, let your mind react. Don't think about any of your fundamentals or anything like that. Just try to be a player and, yeah, just try it again. It's either get rid of the ball before he gets there/she gets there, or it's run away and try to buy some time that way, which I don't have the luxury of doing.

AnnaSofia: How do QBs know at what point in the route to release the ball and how do they learn to trust that the receiver is going to be there at that point in the route?

Jared: What we talk about a lot is called an "indicator step." So, if your receiver is running, let's just say a slant, a three-step slant, that third step should be a little bit more animated by them, a little bit more demonstrative, letting you know, like, I am cutting right now. And we talk about that a lot in the NFL, where I tell St. Brown, say, "Hey man, I need to see that step because then I'll be able to anticipate it a little bit better." Whereas if he doesn't give me that step, I'm not sure if he's going to take one more revolution to break in or break out. But when I do see that step and maybe that head nod toward that step to go, I'm able to anticipate it. The amount of reps we've had together. I know what that step looks like for him, and he knows what I'm looking for. So he's able to give that to me as his indicator step. And it is just a lot of reps, but yes, it allows me to play with a little bit better timing and speed.

AnnaSofia: I guess that's like the point in practice where you get to really recognize how they run and how they do their routes. And you'll see quarterbacks sometimes in flag football release the ball really late, and it ends up being a jump ball, 50-50 for the receiver and the defender. What are some tips for receivers to create space between them and the defender so that you can see that they're open and you can see that window open up?

Jared: I think part of it is that indicator being able to separate with more of a firm step. If that makes sense, instead of rounding it in there, rounding it out, being able to take a very clean, firm jab in or out. And then I think using your body, using your hands. Defensive pass interference is called a lot. I don't think offensive pass interference is called very much. And I think you can use those rules to your advantage. And certainly if your hand is low on their hip, you can kind of get away with some low push-offs. And you can kind of get away with that.

I think if you're a bigger body, you can really use your body to your advantage. We talk about it with tight ends all the time. I'll tell [Sam] LaPorta, just like run into the guy, and that'll get you open just by being physical with them. And so, yeah, you can use your own size to your advantage or you can use your own speed to your advantage, whichever one you have is better.

AnnaSofia: As a quarterback, is there anything you can do to eliminate options before the snap?

Jared: Yeah, another great question. I think you're looking for coverage indicators, and we all kind of know what man coverage looks like—guys across the board covering their guys. And so, if you know it's man coverage, you probably know, "All right, this route's probably not good here, but this one is good." You're able to lower your options from four or five guys to two or three, and your chances of success will go way up.

WURK WURK WURK

With those inside tips from one of the world's top QBs, I want us to be ready physically to play our positions, and play without injury! I am really excited because we also have a top-notch trainer who's going to help us up our game. His main goal is to protect athletes from dangerous injuries and to keep those muscles strong. Brad Davidson is the CEO of The Weight Room in Newport Beach, California. He has trained so many first-round draft picks (like Joe Burrow!) and NFL players, and helps them get to their peak performance. So, in this chapter and the next, Brad is going to give us specific exercises for each position.

In this guide, I want to give you access to the best of the best and the highest-level training for those of you who are very committed to the sport. I also understand that not everyone has access to gym equipment. So, for each position, I am also going to give you fun skill-building options that anyone can do at home or with their friends. These fun exercises have been customized for us by health and fitness expert Scott Jansen.

The exercises in this book are for educational purposes only and are not medical advice. They were recommended by trained professionals, but always check with a doctor or certified trainer before starting any new workout—especially if you have health concerns or injuries. If you're under 18, talk to a parent, guardian, or coach before doing any exercises.

The author and publisher are not responsible for any injuries that may result from using this information.

Listen to your body and be smart.

TEAMMATE SPOTLIGHT--SHAKE AND BAKE

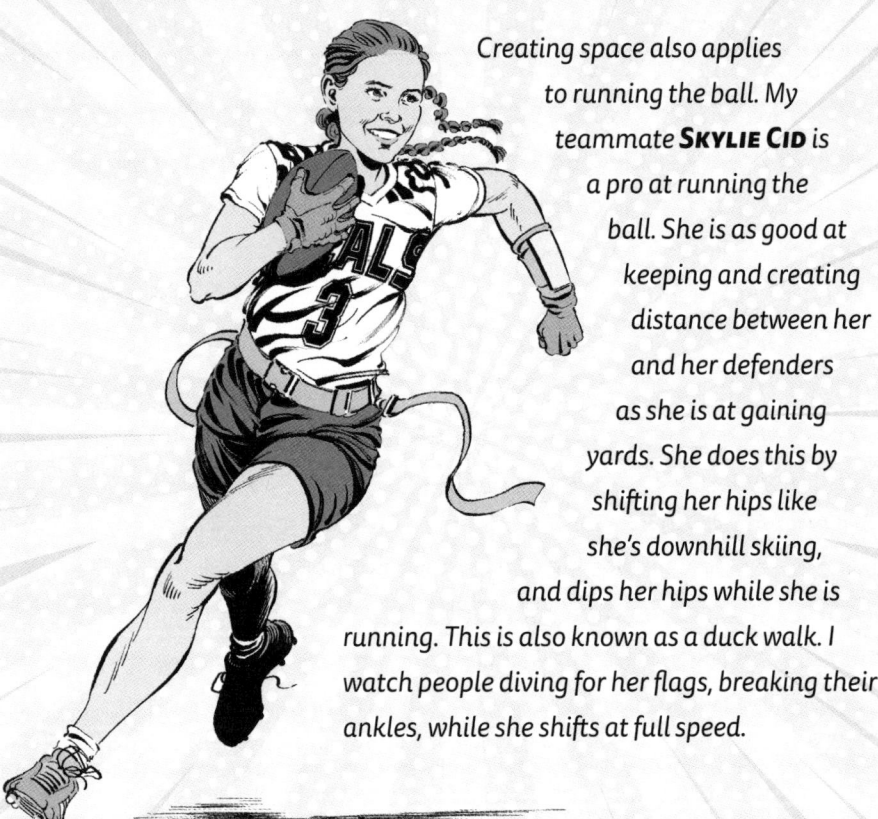

Creating space also applies to running the ball. My teammate **SKYLIE CID** is a pro at running the ball. She is as good at keeping and creating distance between her and her defenders as she is at gaining yards. She does this by shifting her hips like she's downhill skiing, and dips her hips while she is running. This is also known as a duck walk. I watch people diving for her flags, breaking their ankles, while she shifts at full speed.

Quarterback Training

Brad Davidson: When it comes to training quarterbacks, a really big focus has to be on shoulder protection. There's so much movement going forward with the shoulder over and over that if you don't care for the shoulder properly, you'll have pain and issues. So we like to focus on two areas.

1. **Rotator Cuff**
   a) Hands at the belly button, keep the elbow close to your side.
   b) Open up fast.
   c) Control it back slowly to the belly button.

2. **Scapula**
   a) Rest your head on an inclined bench or the top of a chair. Hold the weight in one hand.
   b) Pull your shoulder in to "set the scapula."
   c) With a straight arm, do a diagonal fly movement.
   d) Lower the arm back down.

These two exercises will keep you safe from injury and will allow you to generate more force in the throwing motion so you can throw the ball harder.

Quarterback Fun Training

Dodgeball: Dodgeball is like a school recess version of *The Hunger Games*. Grab your friends and make two teams. Throw a bunch of balls in the middle. When the game starts, sprint to the center, grab a ball and start chucking balls at people like your life depends on it! Duck, spin, and weave to survive. Without even thinking about it, you're developing evasive skills and throwing accuracy.

OFFENSIVE TIPS: SEPARATION ON THE FIELD

When the ball is hiked into the quarterback's hands, she needs to see which of her teammates is open. If all she sees are players paired with defenders, she won't feel confident enough to release the ball. You'll need to create space between you and your defender to help the QB see that you're open.

Here's why you need to create space:

1. **Quarterback Visibility:** When you create space between you and your defender by accelerating,

you are a more visible and attractive target for your quarterback.

2. **Reduce the Risk of Interceptions or Deflections:** When the defenders have tight coverage on you, they increase the chance of them blocking, deflecting, or intercepting the ball. You get a clearer shot at catching the ball correctly and securely when you have more space.
3. **More Time to Run:** With more space, you get more time to make moves and gain yards after catching the ball as you run.

CENTER TIPS

Centers are often underestimated, but they perform a crucial role. They start every play by snapping the ball to the quarterback.

1. **Practice Accuracy**—It goes without saying that if you snap the ball over your QB's head into the sky, your team will lose the down. That down may cost you the series or the game. So if you can find someone to snap to at home, it will make a huge difference on the field. Have a sibling catch your snaps over and over. Set a number for how many snaps you're going to do per day. Even 10 snaps per day is 3,650 more snaps per year!
2. **Practice Routes**—Like wide receivers, you'll need to make sharp cuts and run fast routes. Some coaches

choose to use their centers for long routes and some use their centers for short routes.

3. **Avoid the Rusher**—One thing that is a *crucial* part of being center is avoiding the rusher. Avoid the rusher at all costs! In most club games, the rule is that the rusher has to run in a straight line to the QB, and you have to avoid that line. If you don't, it will be called "impeding the rusher," and you get a penalty. If your assigned route is standing in place and not moving, which is "blocking," then if the rusher bumps into you it's not your fault. But if you have a route that's headed anywhere near the rusher, try to take a step to the right or left (depending on which way your route is), and continue your route from there so then you can still run your route but around the rusher. Something I like to do is kind of give away my route a little bit by facing the direction I'm going. That way, the rusher sees which way I am going and starts rushing from the other side. Usually the rusher lines up a step to the right or a step to the left so they have a straight line to the QB, so you can use that to decide to go the opposite way for the start of your route. When you have to run a route and there is a rusher coming, it's important to make sure your reaction time is quick and that you are running off the line fast. Some leagues let you get in the way of the rusher, and I don't need to tell you how to do that! But usually you have to make sure you avoid the rusher.

Receiver Training

Brad Davidson: For wide receivers, for running backs—I call them skill positions—ACL and knee injuries are some of the greatest risks because there's so much planting and changing direction. When it comes to protecting the ACL, this is where female athletes have greater risk of injury than male athletes. Female athletes have a little wider hip-to-knee ratio, so they need more stabilization of the knee. So I like the Poliquin step-up:

1. **Poliquin Step-up**
   a) Stand with one foot on an incline step so your heel is elevated. Slightly turn your toe out about 30 degrees. Hold a set of weights in your hands. With the other foot, line its heel up with the toe of your first foot. Stand up tall.
   b) Lift your heel off the ground.
   c) Set it back down (15–20 reps).
   This isolates the VMO muscle and the glute muscle to help stabilize the knee.

2. **Kneeling Hamstring Curl**
   a) Curl one leg fast up.
   b) Control it slowly down.
   If you make the hamstring strong, the glute, and the VMO muscle strong, you'll have a much stronger knee and less likelihood of hurting your ACL when you play.

Receiver Fun Training

Ultimate Frisbee: Take soccer, football, and basketball and mix them around in a bowl—that's ultimate frisbee. It's fast-paced and requires lots of cutting, juking, and acceleration to catch those flying discs. When you catch that disc one-handed like Odell Beckham Jr., you gotta stop running and throw it forward. Catch it in the other team's end zone and you can celebrate!

CHAPTER 8.
Hips Don't Lie—Defense

Let's talk about defense in football. No, the other futbol—I mean soccer! I'm sure many of you have grown up playing it. One of the greatest Cinderella stories in sports happened all because of defense. Greece shocked the whole world by winning the UEFA Euro 2004. The odds of them winning were 150-to-1. In fact, they had never even won a major tournament before this one—talk about underdogs! In the Euro 2004, they rarely had possession of the ball, but when they stopped their opponents defensively, they attacked quickly in transition. Greece created defensive walls and scored most of their goals from free kicks and corner kicks. As a soccer player, I know how important defense is, because every offensive position transitions into a defensive position in a matter of seconds. So in both soccer and flag football, defense can shift momentum quickly and break another team down mentally.

TIPS FOR DEFENDERS

1. **Keep your Balance:** Balance helps you move in either direction fast. One way to stay balanced is to keep your feet wide, about shoulder distance.
2. **Get Ready for Movement:** Keep your eyes on your opponent's shoulders, hips, and belly button. The direction her body is facing or where her head and shoulders turn to glance gives you clues to where she plans on running.
3. **Keep a Little Space:** Make sure there's a little space between you and your opponent. If you're close, she can sidestep you and if you're too far, she's got room to cut past you or get away.
4. **Use Two Hands:** With two hands, you have a greater chance of pulling the flag. If she jukes or dodges you, you are covering more area with both hands stretched out.
5. **Get Low:** Break your player down while wrapping your arms around her waist. Attack at the hip! When my brother coached the boys team that I played on, he

yelled, "No flower picking!"—meaning don't reach for a flag like you are picking flowers.

6. **Angles Aren't Just for Math Class:** Try approaching the runner at an angle and force them into areas with less space. As my OC Seals coach Jason Guyser always says, "Safeties should never let anyone behind them." When someone has the ball and is running, try to force them to the inside where you have more numbers, more teammates that can help you grab that flag and stop the runner.

7. **Notice Patterns:** A great shortcut to getting better is to study your opponent and notice patterns. Keep watch of how your opponents evade flag pulls and then strategize from there. Does your player juke you and run down the sideline every time? Sometimes players will look where they are headed, and sometimes quarterbacks will only throw it to a certain side. Coach Guyser always tells us to be on the lookout for patterns because sometimes it's very easy to tell what play is happening next just by paying close attention. If you play center linebacker, your main job is the middle of the field and any short routes or runs in front of you. At this position, you want to make sure you are watching the quarterback's eyes and noticing patterns and movements to make it easier to pull a flag or intercept the throw.

Defensive Training

Our trainer from The Weight Room, Brad Davidson, says, "Defensive players that need to backpedal can practice driving the body backward, basically overloading yourself going backward."

1. **Sled Work**
   a) Put a waist belt on that hooks you to a gym sled, called the "tank." Lean back slightly and give a slight bend to your knees.
   b) Walk backwards by driving the heel down.
   c) Extend the front leg straight as you step backward with the other leg.

   Here's another great exercise for defensive players helping them jump for those interceptions:

2. **Jump Squats**
   a) Stand with feet shoulder-width apart and knees slightly bent.
   b) Go down into a squat with knees bent.
   c) Leap off the floor (swing your arms up with your body, not downward).
   Start with 3–5 reps, and gradually increase the number as your legs get stronger.

Defensive Fun Training

Basketball—Basketball defense is a lot like flag football. You anticipate passes, cut off an offensive player's path, and disrupt plays. Everything happens fast and there's tons of lateral movement. So grab your neighbors and get a pick-up game going! And if you can steal the ball from someone doing a crossover, you can for sure steal flags.

RUSHERS

There is one position on the field where, if you do it right, you could totally change the entire game. That position is the rusher. As a rusher, your goal is to make the quarterback's life miserable. This could mean batting down the ball when they try to throw, pulling their flag, getting in their way, or even scaring them and putting pressure on them. At the start of each play, the rusher who is on defense lines up seven yards from the line of scrimmage, ready to run for her life. When the ball is snapped, the rusher runs as fast as they can toward the QB. Being a rusher can be really simple, but to be an amazing rusher it involves tons of practice and quick decision-making. All the rusher has to do is get in the quarterback's head and shut them down. By doing this you can stop so many of the other team's plays in one game. That can win you many games if you have it down right. The other team might even have to change up their plays because of how well you are doing.

When you are running toward the QB, you have to try to pull their flag before they throw the ball. If you do so, the play is dead and the offense loses that down. They also have to take the ball back to where you pulled their flag! Another thing you can do is if the QB already has their arm up to throw, you can hit the ball down to the ground. You just have to avoid hitting their hands or arm because that could be a penalty! You can even hit the ball forward and try to catch it and run for a touchdown or have a teammate catch it and run. That situation has happened to me many times before! One time, my friend Addi Stern was playing rusher and she hit the ball forward as the QB was trying to throw it, and I caught it and ran for a touchdown! Another time, I was playing rusher and when I hit the ball forward my teammate Alexa Rokos caught it and scored a game-winning touchdown to win the tournament! Things like this happen all the time, which shows how game-changing a good rusher can be. Anyway, back to the position.

Another thing you can do besides hitting the ball is just putting your arms up to block the quarterback's line of sight. That could distract them so they throw it poorly or give you a chance to pull their flag. Most quarterbacks, when a rusher gets close to them, try to run away or make a move to get around them so they can throw or run. What you want to do in this situation is box out the quarterback so they have a harder time. What does it look like if you don't? What it looks like is a rusher running full speed and then when the quarterback makes a move, the rusher goes flying past them. You wouldn't have time to turn and make up for it. By then the QB has probably thrown a game-winning pass already! So instead, run full speed, but when you are near the QB, corner them and box them out so they do not know what to do or which way to go. If they go right or left, you are already on top of it! In summary, the rusher makes sure that the quarterback hates them and has a hard time making plays! Here are a couple things you can do to practice being a great rusher:

Rusher Training

Speed Training

Speed—and explosiveness—is a big part of being a rusher. You have to be super fast to close the gap to the QB before they throw! For very specific training that makes you progressively faster, watch my entire session with trainer Brad Davidson on @annasofiadickens on YouTube. Our expert Scott Jansen recommends the following:

1. **Box Squats**
   a) With or without a bar on your shoulders, stand with your feet shoulder-width distance apart in front of a box or low chair.
   b) Squat down low, pushing your hips back and keeping your chest up.
   c) Stand back up (repeat 12 reps, 3 sets).

2. **Broad Jumps**
    a) Stand with feet shoulder-width distance apart.
    b) Squat down.
    c) Jump as far forward as possible (repeat 5 times, 3 sets).

Practice and Reps

The more you get used to making quick decisions, the better you are! Practice by having someone pretend to be a QB and make gestures to indicate what they are going to do. You then decide whether to put your arms up, bat down the ball, or pull their flag!

Research

All the best rushers do research on the quarterback they are about to go up against. They notice patterns like what the QB usually does every play or how they react to rushers. This can help you be prepared to dominate!

Rusher Fun Training

Relay Races—Relay races can really enhance acceleration for rushers. Think of it as a fast game of hot potato. You tag your teammate, make the handoff, and that's their chance to fly!

TEAMMATE SPOTLIGHT--THE RUSH QUEEN

My close friend and teammate **ADDI STERN** is one of the best rushers I know. She is no doubt one of the best rushers in the country. In the championships of one of the tournaments we were playing, Addi sacked the QB nine times and batted her ball down six times! She is truly an outstanding rusher because she has so much knowledge in reading the quarterback and what they are about to do, so that she can make quick decisions to beat her! Addi also does tons of speed training, which makes her one of the fastest girls on our team.

UNIVERSAL MOVEMENTS FOR ALL FLAG FOOTBALL PLAYERS

Here are some universal movements recommended by fitness expert Scott Jansen:

While each position in flag football has unique demands, some key foundational exercises benefit all athletes by improving **coordination**, **strength**, **power**, and **injury prevention**. These movements build **a complete athlete**, helping with sprinting efficiency, agility, force absorption, and multi-directional control.

1. **Jumping Rope**—Enhances **foot speed**, **coordination**, and **cardiovascular endurance**.
2. **Bounding**—Develops **explosive power** and **sprint efficiency** by mimicking the force application of running.
3. **Multi-Plane Lunging**—Trains **lower-body strength, flexibility**, and **stability** in **multiple directions**, mimicking game movements.

TEAMMATE SPOTLIGHT-- THE FLAG-PULLING MACHINE

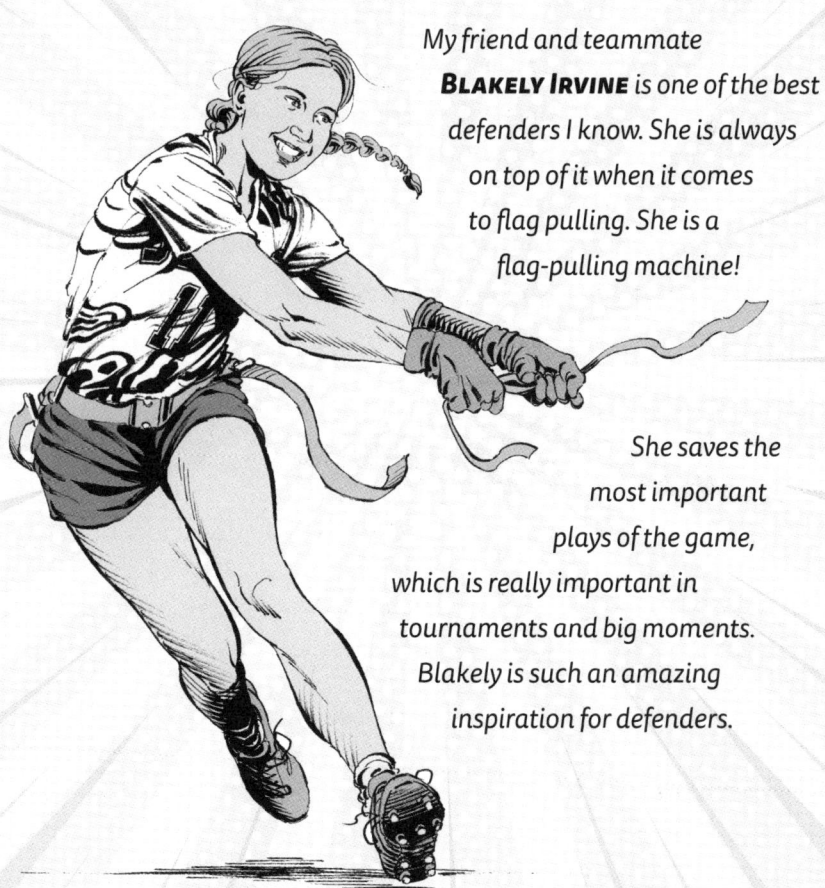

My friend and teammate **BLAKELY IRVINE** is one of the best defenders I know. She is always on top of it when it comes to flag pulling. She is a flag-pulling machine!

She saves the most important plays of the game, which is really important in tournaments and big moments. Blakely is such an amazing inspiration for defenders.

4. **Pushing/Pulling Sleds**—Builds **acceleration power**, **strength**, and **conditioning** in the lower body.
5. **Running with Parachutes**—Strengthens **top-end speed** and **sprint mechanics** by forcing athletes to run with resistance.
6. **Inchworm Walk-Outs to Spider-Man Steps**—Improves **core stability**, **flexibility**, and **mobility**, essential for **preventing injuries**.
7. **Supine Hamstring Walkouts**—Strengthens the **hamstrings** and **glutes**, crucial for **acceleration** and **sprint endurance**.
8. **Single-Leg Romanian Deadlifts (RDLs)**—Enhances **balance, posterior chain strength**, and **single-leg stability**, all essential for **quick directional changes**.

These exercises should be incorporated **regularly** into **warm-ups, conditioning circuits,** and **strength sessions** to build a **well-rounded, resilient athlete**.

CHAPTER 9.

Get Prepped

It's 1985, and future NFL Hall of Famer, Super Bowl champion, *Fox NFL Sunday* analyst, and *Good Morning America* anchor Michael Strahan, is 13 years old, chasing his big brothers around outside his home, an American military base in Mannheim, Germany. Before he was any of the amazing things that we now know him for, he was just a fun-loving kid who loved to eat his mom's cakes and pies. I mean, *loved*. Chocolate lava cake, black forest cake, mixed berry pies, cherry pies, you name it. One afternoon, Strahan notices his brothers' friends calling him Bob: "Bob! Bob! Keep up, Bob!" At first he thinks it's just a dumb nickname. I mean, can you think of all the brutal things your big brother has called *you*? But then one day, someone breaks it to him that BOB is an acronym that stands for "Booty on Back." Newsflash: they were calling him fat!

This is where the story gets good. And I was lucky enough to get a one-on-one interview with Michael Strahan for us to hear his story firsthand. I wanted to know how a kid on a military base far from America who loves eating cakes and pies ends up a celebrated pro football player and one of the most hard-working and successful people in television. Here's some of the interview:

Michael: Oh, you know, I used to eat a lot. I ate a lot, I eat a lot. My nickname was Bob, it meant "Booty on Back." I had a big old butt. So that's what made me work out. I started doing these [exercises]. Jane Fonda was big back then, and she had these VHS tapes you put in and there were a bunch of leg lifts and butt exercises.

AnnaSofia: Like the dancing ones?

Michael: Well, I didn't have the leg warmers, but…yeah, I had everything except for the leg warmers and the tights. But, yeah, Jane Fonda, you got it. That's who it was. So I used to do her videos. And then that football player I talked about, Herschel Walker, he was known to do pushups and sit-ups without weights. So I did a lot of pushups and sit-ups and I did a lot of leg lifts with Jane Fonda. But I would watch TV with my parents, and then every time a commercial came on, I'd get on the floor and I'd do my exercises, then watch the show, every commercial. And my dad saw me doing that for like six months, and he realized I was really committed to working off my big old butt. So he started going to the gym with me when I was 13 and completely transformed my body, my…everything, my belief in myself, just everything.

MICHAEL STRAHAN

AnnaSofia: I mean, that's discipline. Getting down on the commercials. Some commercials are like 10 minutes long. Have you seen the ones that are like six or more commercials?

Michael: Tell me about it. Exactly. But I was committed because I wanted to work off that big old butt. I was committed. I didn't want to be made fun of anymore.

AnnaSofia: You're so amazing at managing your day. I remember coming to get to hang out with you while you were hosting

GET PREPPED

Good Morning America, and you were like, "Want to come next door? I'm hosting $100,000 *Pyramid*"...

Michael: Ha!

AnnaSofia: ...and then you jumped on a plane to go to Fox Sports! For teen athletes that are busy, what's the key to managing your time?

Michael: Yeah, have good people around you who tell you where to be and kind of point you in the direction and say, I really do have to have people like that. I have an amazing group who work with me to keep me organized. But I also think you have to, I hate to say it like this, but for me, because I have to wake up so early and I have so much stuff to do and my mind always has to be present. I have to be selfish sometimes. I have to say no. I have to miss some things that don't seem to be fun. I'm not out late at dinners during the week. If anything, I very rarely go out to dinner unless it's a Friday or Saturday. So, I have to just be very disciplined about how I spend my time and make sure that I make the most of it. So, for me spending my time at home with my family, hanging out, kids, nothing gets better than that. That's better than any party I've ever gone to. And I'm glad that I kind of had a chance to do all those things before I got these jobs because it's out of my system, anyway. But just being very disciplined and saying no, if it's something that I feel is just gonna impede or make my next day, make me tired or whatever. Just say, nope, I'm good.

AnnaSofia: Yeah, and you wake up early, but hey, you Wake Up Happy.

Michael: I wake up happy—you got the book!—you know that's right, Wake Up Happy, baby.

AnnaSofia: And I love that especially as a singer because I wake up every morning with my favorite songs to get me going for the day and I make sure that every time before I go to bed, I play the piano and I kind of wind the whole day down.

Michael: Wow!

AnnaSofia: I bring the level down and I do that every single night even if my whole family gets mad at me for playing really late.

Michael: Let 'em get mad.

AnnaSofia: It's worth it because it makes me decompress and it's really nice. So I love that because I do the same thing.

Michael: And I tell you what, though, you know what? Trust me, they like it when you play the piano. And one day when you're off in college and that piano's not playing, they're gonna be missing you. Trust me, I miss my girls here at home. But it is really something, and I agree with you, music is so important to me. I start my day with music, on the car to work with music, when I get into my dressing room, I'm just listening to music before I do any show. And I just love it. It just puts you in the right frame of mind, in the right mood. I wish I could play the piano. I actually took piano lessons and I wasn't bad, but my fingers were so jacked up from football, I was hitting two or three keys. Look at that, see? See how that finger bends like that? That's not very good for pianos. So if your parents or your siblings get mad at you for playing piano at your house, you're more than welcome to come play piano at my house any day.

AnnaSofia: Oh, my gosh, yeah, I see it. I'd love to. And if you're always listening to music, put my songs on your playlist.

Michael: I got it. I gotcha. I'm downloading the second I get done.

AnnaSofia: Do you have any advice on mental discipline for teen athletes on or off the field?

Michael: Yeah, I mean, I think mental discipline is one thing that I learned when I was Bob "Booty on Back," big old butt Michael. I learned that discipline was the key to making my life what I wanted it to be, because we all have some things or something that we don't like, something that we want to learn, something that we want to create. A lot of people have great ideas and have the same ambitions, but a lot of people just don't have the desire. They don't have the ability to stick with it or they don't want to stick with it. They don't see the big picture. So in order to, in my opinion, accomplish what you want to accomplish, you have to see where you want to go. You have to picture that end zone and just everything in between is worth it to get to that point. I mean, I'm living proof of that in my life. I look at where I started and where I wanted to go and I just work without even consciously thinking about how hard the work was. Because I knew what the end result that I wanted was. And in all instances where I've done it, it's always worked out. But you have to be disciplined. Discipline means waking up. Discipline means sometimes doing the same thing every day, like playing the piano, because it's part of your routine that makes you better. And I found that the guys or the girls who can stick with it, who are the most disciplined, always seem to be the ones who always have the most success. Because they know that they're prepared for any moment that's thrown their way because they have the discipline, they have the desire, they have the drive to work their way through anything. And if you have somebody who's lazy, who drops off, and doesn't have the discipline, that tends to be the person who lives with regrets. And that's something that I never want to live with.

AnnaSofia: That's so inspiring. And discipline, it also takes sacrifice. You have to sacrifice so many things that you want to be doing. But at the end of the day, it's "Where do you want to be in life?"

Michael: And it's very hard, though, when you're a teenager, for me being 13, 14, 15, 16 years old, working out with my dad in the gym on the weekends when I know other kids are out riding a bike, having fun, hanging out. And mine was a very disciplined childhood, but my dad didn't do that because I asked him or because he demanded it. He did it because he saw how disciplined I was in front of the TV. So he just carried that over to the gym. So I wasn't going to say to my dad, no, I don't want it anymore. I was like, okay, hunker down and get this done. And my dad said something to me in the gym one day, we were working out. He could just tell that I was being a kid. I was just kind of not there mentally. He looked and he said, "Son, just focus. And I promise you one day it'll pay off." I didn't know what he was talking about. I'm living in Germany. I'm not even playing football. But I just think that that discipline has helped me in every aspect of my life. As a football player, when other guys wanted to go home and didn't wanna do the extra work as far as lifting weights or doing extra sprints, I was gonna be the guy. When it comes to the discipline of taking care of your body as a professional athlete, a lot of guys neglect that because, eh, it fixed itself. No, I was disciplined enough to do that. When it's waking up in the morning, you go to *GMA* [hosting *Good Morning America*] and consistently try to be great every single day because you have to remember, and which I try to think about, it may be my thousandth day doing a job, but it may be someone else's first time ever seeing me do it. So you have to approach it with the same energy, as if this is the first time someone could see me do this job and I never want to disappoint anybody. Being able to be prepared for all those things requires a lot of discipline in your life. And you do miss a lot of things, but at the end of the day, you work hard while you're young, you enjoy it a lot more when you get older.

AnnaSofia: That's an incredible perspective on it. Like this is someone's first time watching me do it. That can apply to so many things in life. That's really cool. Something I've learned is that you're not what you do, you're what you do every day. So I make sure that I do what I love to do every single day, get in habits, routines.

Michael: Yep. And that is so important. And you know, be humble. No matter what success level you have, be humble. And when you have your first day at doing something, say you get a new job or you're trying out for a new team or you're in a new class or whatever it may be, a lot of people get so intimidated because they're like, I've never done this before. You have to think about it that everybody's had a first day. You know, everybody's had that anxiety of being their first time in the middle of something. Even the person who's an expert in something, they had just had the discipline of working hard from day one when they weren't an expert and they were a beginner in order to develop the expertise. That goes in every aspect of your life. Everybody had the first day, just continue to work hard and you can develop into an expert in anything you put your mind to.

AnnaSofia: Exactly. Yeah, that's great. Well, this has been so amazing. Thank you so much for talking with me.

Michael: All right, you know what? It is my pleasure anytime, and one day you teach me to play the piano.

AnnaSofia: I will, with nine of your fingers.

Michael: All right, deal.

TIME MANAGEMENT

Managing your time is an important skill to have, especially if you have multiple commitments. I'm not saying that I have it all together because, trust me, I definitely struggle with managing my time. But here are a few things that I've learned coming from someone who does play multiple sports at a time. There are always going to be things that distract you. Life is full of distractions, left and right. But you need to learn how to block out those distractions and stay on track. Sure, it can be good to get a little distracted once in a while to get your mind off of things and reset. Sometimes I feel like life would be so much easier if I just did whatever I wanted and relaxed or watched my favorite TV shows. Or I could say stuff like, "I'll just get it done tomorrow." But after a while, tomorrow isn't an option anymore. That life of putting things off might be easier in the short term, but is it better? Don't you want to be something big and be the best you can be? Don't you want to be better than you were yesterday and be the strongest version of yourself? That life comes with way more benefits than you think. You also need to get into good habits, which I will talk about in a little.

GETTING QUALITY SLEEP

Getting good sleep is also another thing that can change your life dramatically. It transforms you into a better person. I agree with this because I know when I get bad sleep I am so cranky the next day. Quality sleep allows your body to fix and repair itself. Sleeping strengthens your immune system and enhances things like focus, memory, and decision-making. It also makes you a happier person when you get quality sleep. Who doesn't want to be a happier person? You become more patient and empathetic toward people you care about. For athletes, it's vital for recovery and performance. If you are in a stage of deep sleep, your body goes through processes like muscle repair, tissue growth, and the release of growth hormones, which are good for athletes. You improve your strength, endurance, and your overall performance. Getting good sleep is such an easy way to make you better in many ways. I also just love sleeping and can't get up until I'm dragged out of bed, so I don't mind when someone tells me I have to sleep more or go to bed earlier.

If you are someone who has school sports and club sports and just all of the things, I understand how challenging it can be. Instead of waking up thinking, "Ugh, this week is so hard and tomorrow is so hard," try to only think about the day you are in. Go through your schedule in your head, whether that's school, practices, lessons, etc. When you are going through your schedule, think about what specific times in the day you're going to have rest time and free time so you don't catch yourself debating if you should skip one of your practices or important things you actually need to do. This way you will have structure in your day and be more relaxed and comfortable about the long days you have ahead of you. Going to practice can be fun, but for some people it's not always the most fun. So if thinking about practice is scary, then think about what you will reward yourself with afterward, like a warm shower or a movie. Make sure you never procrastinate on your homework either, because as an athlete coming back from night practices and getting home around 9:00 or 10:00, it's hard to get all your homework done, so try to do it earlier in the day or right when you get home. Trust me, it's way better having free time after doing all of your responsibilities than having free time before with all of the stuff you need to do just sitting there in the back of your mind. All those tasks left undone can weigh on you.

If you schedule things and have structure in your life, everything becomes way easier. I know it's hard also having side responsibilities as well. First, you have to make sure your household chores and responsibilities are finished along with your schoolwork. My chores are cleaning the kitchen on all days and doing the dishes a few days per week for our big family. And I'm supposed to keep my room clean. My brain feels

clearer and I become more creative when I'm writing music in my room if my room is clean. Try to stay clean because a clean room allows for a clear mind. If all your chores and responsibilities are checked off, then it makes it so much easier to schedule extra training practices or hangouts with your friends! There are so many things in my life like music or sports that make me have to skip some school, which makes it even harder for me to stay on top of things. Something you can do is talk to your teachers and figure out a way together for you to stay on top of it all and get it done. Teachers generally want the same thing as you—they want you to succeed in their class and they want to see that you care about succeeding. So have a conversation with them if you know you're going to miss school time.

MAKING YOURSELF BETTER

A thought you should constantly be having is "How can I make myself better?" That can mean as a person, athlete, or friend. When you are working out, think about how you can make it the best workout to make you the best. When you find yourself in a situation that gives you an opportunity to be a better friend or sibling, take it. For example, one time my mom made me walk home from my soccer practice because she couldn't take me home. I was so annoyed but then I thought, how can I optimize this time and make use of it? So I decided to walk on the straights and run up the hills. By doing that I got a workout in for the day and made use of the time to make myself better. Soon after you create structure in your life, you start to realize you want your free time to turn into time you can use to make yourself better at something you love. Working hard and getting better becomes like an addiction. You just get so addicted to working hard, and it's such a great feeling.

GOOD HABITS

Making good habits can dramatically transform your life with structure and consistency. If you establish daily routines like making your bed, eating healthy meals, exercises, sports training, and prioritizing sleep, you win better physical and mental health. Have you ever noticed that when you're rested and your room is clean, your day feels like it just flows? These habits start to replace stress and help you become more productive and motivated. Keeping up with consistent good habits helps you stay focused on your goals and also advances you to where you want to be in life way faster. By committing to positive habits, you set yourself on a path that only leads you forward and not backward. Ultimately, it gives you a higher chance of achieving your long-term goals, so why not take that chance?

CHAPTER 10.
It Ain't Over 'til It's Over

Sorry, guys. But I gotta give you one more Patriots example. Because my mom's side of the family is in Massachusetts, my brother Sam-Reed became a huge Patriots fan. When Tom Brady would play a big game back when Sam-Reed was 10 years old, he would take his framed posters off the wall and build a candlelit shrine to Brady around our TV set. It was normal to walk into the living room on a Sunday morning and see this huge shrine to the G.O.A.T., even before people started calling him that.

Whether you like or dislike the Patriots or Bucs, Brady did teach us that it ain't over 'til it's over. I heard an interview where players said there's nothing scarier than playing against Tom Brady, especially when you see him sitting on the bench with his head in his hands when his team is behind. It can only mean one thing to see him like that—he's cooking up revenge in his brain! I will never forget one of the greatest comebacks in Super Bowl history when the Patriots overcame being down 28–3 against the Atlanta Falcons. Before the comeback had even started, wide receiver Julian Edelman said to his teammate Brady, "This is gonna make a great story." These guys already knew that it was possible to make a comeback. And spoiler alert, the Patriots came back to win Super Bowl LI 34–28. Their determination and optimism won them the game. The lesson is, no matter what situation you're in, never stop playing your hardest until the very end. And don't stop believing!

DON'T STOP 'TIL YOU HEAR THE WHISTLE

When it comes to learning girls flag football, keep this in mind every time you run the ball. Every week at Friday Night Lights, our nighttime games, I see girls catch the ball and either slow down or stop running completely because they think their flag has been pulled or they've stepped out of bounds. Girl, it ain't over 'til it's over! If you hadn't slowed down or stopped, you might have gotten a lot more yards, maybe even a touchdown!

TEAMMATE SPOTLIGHT-- TEARS DON'T MEAN IT'S OVER

Many of my teammates are on the same travel soccer team together, so we've been through lots of ups and downs. One time we were in the semifinals of a multi-state tournament and we were losing with 10 seconds left. It was bone-chilling cold with crazy winds, and we were actually crying. We had fought so hard. My football and soccer teammate **AVERY OLSON** fired the ball across half the field and scored the craziest buzzer beater I've ever seen to tie the game! We won in a PK shootout and went on to win the tournament. You never know what can happen, so just keep playing!

IT AIN'T OVER 'TIL IT'S OVER

No one in the current game knows about coming back like the guy they call "Captain Comeback," Los Angeles Rams quarterback Matthew Stafford. I had a chance to sit down with him to talk, and here's a small excerpt from the interview. You can watch the whole thing on my website, annasofiadickens.com, and YouTube channel, @annasofiadickens.

AnnaSofia: It doesn't get any cooler than the guy we're talking with today. Matthew Stafford is an NFL Super Bowl champion. He's the King of Comebacks. Stafford was once the face of the Detroit Lions and now he's the hero of the LA Rams. He's literally rewriting the quarterback legacy playbook one clutch throw at a time.

Matthew: Hey, thanks for having me. I appreciate it.

AnnaSofia: Yes, of course! What was it like winning the Super Bowl with the Rams and how do you deal with pressure from an audience that's, like, half the world?

Matthew: Winning the Super Bowl was pretty cool. It was an amazing thing. Obviously, it was my first season here. I got traded to LA in 2021 and just was going to treat it as a new beginning. Nothing more than that.

We had a great collection of players and coaches and a group that was able to kind of pull it together and obviously succeed and win the Super Bowl in my first season, which was an incredible feeling and incredible feat, and we've been

MATTHEW STAFFORD

trying to get back there ever since. And since we're talking about pressure, there was definitely some in that season. I think the biggest thing for me is just relying on the people around me. I have so many great people in my family. I've got friends, teammates, coaches that have all helped me out. You can't go through life, go through a season without those people and without their help. And so I'm lucky to be surrounded by a bunch of good ones and they helped me along the way.

IT AIN'T OVER 'TIL IT'S OVER

AnnaSofia: What's one thing about being an NFL quarterback that the fans don't realize?

Matthew: I think probably our weekly preparation. They get to see the final product on Sunday and they get to see us go out there and play a game. We either win or we lose. We play well or we play poorly. But there's so much that goes into it, not only from a physical standpoint but a mental standpoint as well. And then there's the balance, at least in my life, of okay, I've got this job that is pressure-packed and I'm responsible to a lot of people in that job. But I also have four daughters and a wife and I'm really responsible to them as well. So there's just a lot of balancing that goes on to try to figure out what the right recipe is to go out there, play well, and still do all the things I want to do in life.

AnnaSofia: I talk a lot about health and nutrition in my book. Do you have a go-to meal for your game days?

Matthew: I usually keep it pretty simple. If we're playing a 1:00 o'clock game, you know, I will just have eggs, bacon, and a piece of toast or something like that, some fruit in the morning. If it's a night game, [it's] usually chicken, brown rice, broccoli. Pretty boring. I try to keep it simple. I don't have a huge appetite on game day until the game's over. Then I'm usually pretty hungry.

AnnaSofia: Yeah, I mean that sounds good anyway. I bet you have some great people making it like really good. I also have a chapter in my book about comebacks, and I've heard that people call you "Captain Comeback." You have more than 35 fourth-quarter comebacks, and that's one of the highest in NFL history. What's your favorite comeback story?

Matthew: Technically, the Super Bowl win was a comeback. That's probably the one that sticks out the most. There are ones that are probably a few more points here or there. But that one meant the most, obviously the most on the line in that game.... I love those moments. I relish having the ball in my hand. I hate being on the sideline and having your defense have to make a play.... I'd rather have it in my hands and, win or lose, I'll take the heat if we lose. But it's a lot of fun. Would love to be up in the fourth quarter by two scores, but it's the NFL! There are so many competitive games. We've got to find ways to win them at the end, and I've been lucky to be a part of teams that have done that.

AnnaSofia: Yeah, and it's also a lot of pressure. You're probably the type of person who wants to be in control of the play because you are the quarterback, but it's also a lot of pressure because you can either bring it back or you [blow it]...

Matthew: Yeah!

AnnaSofia: Yeah, you know, when I saw you a couple days ago, we were talking about how you were at the US Select Team flag football tryout that I was at. What are your thoughts on girls flag football and where do you see the sport a couple years from now?

Matthew: It's amazing. To be honest with you, going to that tryout was pretty eye-opening for me. Not just in numbers, but also in ability.... I was really, really impressed with yourself and a bunch of other people who were out there running around. So it was really cool to see that. I think it's grown exponentially in a short amount of time. I imagine it's going to continue to do that.

CHAPTER 11.
The Future of Flag

THE TAYLOR SWIFT EFFECT

Whether you're a bracelet-wearing Swiftie or not, you can't deny the huge effect that Taylor Swift had in the growth of flag football. Hear me out. Taylor isn't just a pop star. Her Eras Tour is considered the biggest live music event in history. Just by showing up to perform, she can change the economy of an entire country! We're football players and we like stats, right? Let's break down Taylor's stats. New data cited in *Newsweek* shows that the Eras Tour, which hit 19 countries, grew the global economy by over $9 billion. Let's look at Los Angeles alone. With six shows, the U.S. Travel Association reported that the city of LA made $320 million, creating 3,300 jobs. Think about it, almost every fan who buys tickets also spends money on local restaurants, hotels, driver services, and tour merch—all those bracelets and sweatshirts. Even Amazon and Etsy sellers get a big boost when fans buy the non-official stuff. Picture this in every city. The spending that happened for each one of her shows in that city was the same as if that city hosted a Super Bowl. Except Taylor has hosted nearly 150 Super Bowls! We also saw that Taylor can move her fans to action in politics. When she posted, encouraging her fanbase to register to vote, there were 35,000 registrations in a single day.

Now take that firepower that can change a country's finances and politics, and apply it to our favorite sport. When Taylor Swift started a relationship with Kansas City Chiefs tight end Travis Kelce, you better believe big things happened! First of all, Kelce's jersey had a 400 percent increase in sales. That means that however many jerseys sold with Kelce's name on the back, his relationship with Taylor caused those sales to go up times five! I guess everyone wants to wear their boyfriend's jersey, and it's like her fanbase all decided he was their man! As for viewership of games, the Kansas City Chiefs owner Clark Hunt said on CNBC's *Mad Money* that female viewership has increased "leaps and bounds" thanks to Taylor and Travis' relationship. His daughter, Gracie Hunt, even estimated a 30–40 percent increase in fans since Taylor's first time attending a game.

Tons of girls all over the world started watching hours of football and got a glimpse of Taylor Swift on the screen for just a couple of minutes. It seems to be a very smart business decision by the NFL and each TV network to show her. But it does make some fans mad because they think it's drawing the spotlight away from the fact that the Chiefs have established a real dynasty in football, with a stretch of dominance only seen a couple times before in history. There was also a trend on TikTok where girls would film guys' reactions to them saying that "Taylor Swift really put Travis Kelce on the map" because they were dating, but this made guys and football fans everywhere furious because they have loved Travis Kelce way longer and claim that he is more famous. The Chiefs have been to five of the last six Super Bowls and got all the way to the AFC Championship Game in that one they missed. I would argue that the Chiefs and the game of football actually benefit from more exposure, whether fans like when the camera pans to her or not. Either way, just having Taylor there inspires so many girls to watch football.

And how about all the girls that picked up a football and started playing flag right when the Taylor Effect happened?

Flag football was announced as an Olympic sport only three weeks after Taylor went to her first Chiefs game, so there was definitely a lot of excitement about girls being able to represent their country. But there's no doubt Taylor got people interested in and talking about American football. Toshane Boyce, the participation coordinator of NFL UK, said "Now Taylor Swift's involvement ramps [participation] up even more. Girls are talking about it and want to get involved. The Taylor effect is helping us massively." One of the players representing Great Britain at the 14U level, Valeria Barrocar La Femina, said that Swift has "brought a whole new crowd to the game."

SPREADING THE GAME

One of my biggest life goals is to spread the game of flag football. That's why I wrote this book in the first place! I want everyone to have an experience like I did playing this amazing game. It is so fulfilling, and I hope that every girl gets to play and feel this level of excitement! Every week I do clinics for girls who want to learn with my good friend Mia Balabanian, who is on my high school team and the US Select Team with me. She is such a good coach because she loves the game just as much as I do and has so much experience learning and playing. I hope that this book inspires you to play your hardest and helps spread the game to the rest of the girls in the world. Boys too!

FUTURE OF FLAG

Football is such a massive industry, brand, and game. There is nobody better at analyzing the future of football than Joel Klatt. He was a record-setting QB for the Colorado Buffaloes, and you can see him breaking down the biggest matchups every weekend on FOX Sports. His expertise is equal to none and he knows almost *too* much about the game. I just got to sit down with him—A Fireside Chat with Joel Klatt! If you want to check it out and learn some cool stuff about how college NIL (name, image, likeness) deals and how transfer portals work, watch it on @annasofiadickens on YouTube. Here is his perspective on the future of the game:

"Anytime you see a sport that's included in the Olympics, you see a massive amount of growth. There are places where young men can go play football. The growth where I see it is on the women's side. I believe that football will become a much bigger part of intercollegiate athletics for women in the flag game at the college level. To me this is the tipping point, and what we're about to see is explosive growth in women's flag football across the nation and in intercollegiate athletics. So much of life is about timing."

Nothing could be more exciting than the timing of the Olympics and how that has affected all levels of the game. I talked with the executive director of NFL Flag Izell Reese at the Oakley Alliance Icon Invitational Tournament to get his take on the growth of the game. Reese, also the CEO of RCX Sports, was a starting safety for the Dallas Cowboys, Denver Broncos, and Buffalo Bills. He told me something I didn't realize, that the number of kids playing flag football is now higher than the OG sport, tackle football: "This sport is here to stay. It's here to be played at all levels, and it's a staple under football now. You have flag and you have tackle, and the numbers are starting to dwarf tackle numbers."

What's even crazier is that the NFL players we have worshipped our whole lives now want to play *our* sport! "When that [Olympic] door opened, you hear NFL players saying they want to play if they get the opportunity. I think you'll continue to see the level of talent internationally continue to grow. What the Olympics solidified is that the sport of flag football is a global game. I'm excited it's happening first on US soil in LA '28, and I don't think it's going to be one and done, there's gonna be skyrocket growth and exposure to come from it."

Just the thought of these giant NFL players competing with flag players who have been amateurs their whole lives is crazy. I'll have to be like "Hey, Tyreek Hill, you may be fast, but you don't know how to dip your hips and drag your ankles like my teammate Skylie Cid!"

Flag football is a game that I will continue to love and hopefully you will too! I hope this guide was useful to you and that you will join me in spreading the world's best game.

About the Author

AnnaSofia Dickens is a fifteen-year-old athlete and singer-songwriter (@annasofiadickens on Instagram, YouTube, and TikTok). Dickens wrote and recorded "We Run This House" at age 14, a pop theme song for the NFL Females in Flag movement, that was played in stadium at the NFL Pro Bowl 2024. As a wide receiver on the USA Football No. 1–ranked 15U women's flag football team, and player on the US Select Team, Dickens' dream is to compete at a D-1 level and represent her country in the Olympics. She hopes to inspire girls from all over the world to play the game that she loves, and was excited to combine her passion of singing and songwriting with her sports. AnnaSofia lives in Southern California with her brothers, sister, and parents, and likes to visit her family's summer home and relatives in Sweden.